DAY FIGHTER ACES OF THE LUFTWAFFE 1943–45

CASEMATE | ILLUSTRATED

CASEMATE | ILLUSTRATED

DAY FIGHTER ACES OF THE LUFTWAFFE 1943–45

NEIL PAGE

CASEMATE | ILLUSTRATED

This work could not have been compiled without the generous and unstinting support and encouragement of Jean-Louis Roba, Erik Mombeek, Jean-Yves Lorant, Dr. Jochen Prien, Michel Ledet, Bernd Barbas, Paul Stipdonk and Michael Meyer. Thank you for saying "no problem."

I should like to dedicate this publication to the veterans who took the time to send photos and reminiscences: Ernst Schröder, Hans Weik, Karl-Heinz von den Steinen, Günther Ehrlich, Friedrich-Wilhelm "Timo" Schenk, Jules Meimberg, and Willi Unger. Thank you. All personal accounts translated by Neil Page.

CIS0018

Print Edition: ISBN 978-1-61200-879-0
Digital Edition: ISBN 978-1-61200-880-6

Design by Battlefield Design
Profiles by Vincent Dhorne
Printed and bound in the Czech Republic by FINIDR, s.r.o.

CASEMATE PUBLISHERS (US)
Telephone (610) 853-9131
Fax (610) 853-9146
Email: casemate@casematepublishers.com
www.casematepublishers.com

CASEMATE PUBLISHERS (UK)
Telephone (01865) 241249
Fax (01865) 794449
Email: casemate-uk@casematepublishers.co.uk
www.casematepublishers.co.uk

Title page: Bf 109 G-6/R6 White 3 flown by Uffz. Franz Stadler, 7./JG 27, Maleme, Crete, April 1944. 7. Staffel was still operating its tropicalized Gustavs ("Trops") in Crete long after the rest of the Geschwader had departed the Mediterranean.

Contents page: A Bf 109 *Kanonenboot*.
Map: The battle of the Bulge. (U.S. Government)

Note: aircraft illustrations and profiles are not to scale.
Note to the reader: Frequently used foreign words, such as unit designations and ranks, and proper nouns are not italicized.

Contents

Timeline of Events

Already on the back foot in the Western Desert, 1943 opened for the Wehrmacht with an ominous portent: by February 2, 1943, the German 6th Army under Field Marshal Paulus had been destroyed at Stalingrad, a loss of almost 250,000 men. From there on, on the Eastern Front—apart from Hitler's despairing throw of the dice with Operation *Citadel*, his massive offensive to close the Kursk salient in July 1943—the retreat to the gates of Berlin was inexorable as it was inevitable. Within a year of Kursk, the beleaguered Germans would be facing the Allies on a bewildering array of fronts: in Italy, in Normandy, in the South of France, and on the vast Eastern Front that stretched from the Baltic to the Black Sea. But it was the hubristic "defense of the Reich," in the skies above the "home front," that went largely unheralded as the ceaseless swarms of USAAF Eight and Fifteenth Air Force B-24 Liberator and B-17 Flying Fortress bombers, and RAF Lancasters pounded to oblivion the *Heimat*, the homeland, night and day, stretching the Luftwaffe to breaking point in terms of machines and pilots.

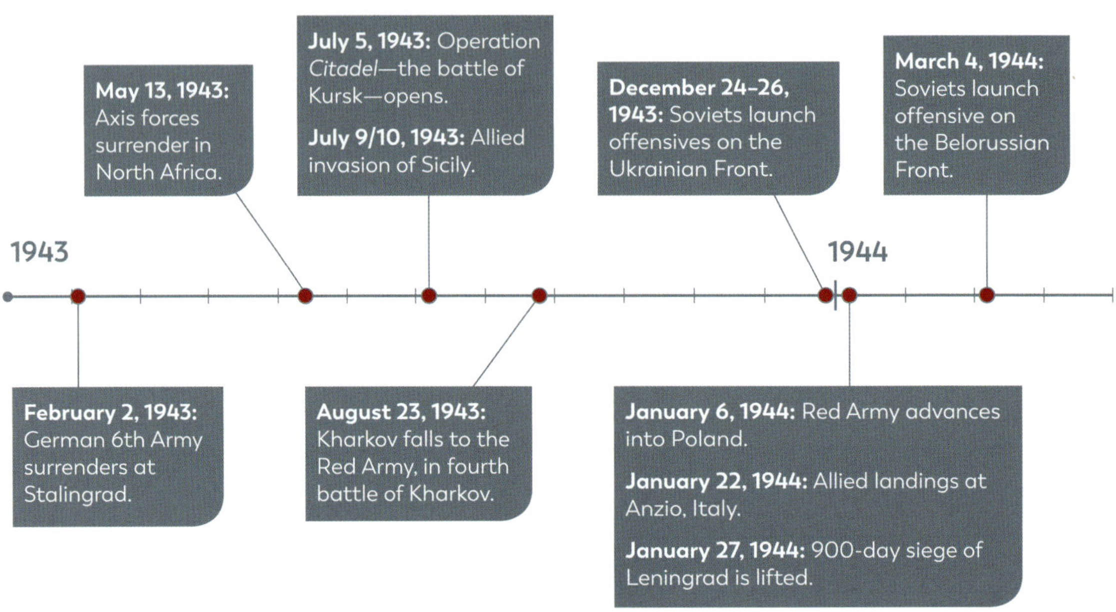

Maj. Siegfried Schnell, a Luftwaffe veteran since 1936 and one of the best scorers in the West, was killed in action on February 25, 1944 as Kommandeur IV./JG 54.

June 5, 1944: Rome falls to the Allies.

June 6, 1944: D-Day, the Allied invasion of Normandy.

June 22, 1944: Operation *Bagration*, the Soviet summer offensive, opens.

August 15, 1944: Operation *Dragoon*, the Allied landings in the South of France.

August 25, 1944: Liberation of Paris.

December 16–27, 1944: Battle of the Bulge, Ardennes.

December 27, 1944: Soviets encircle Budapest.

1945

January 1, 1945: Operation *Bodenplatte*. The Luftwaffe is eviscerated.

March 6, 1945: Final German offensive, to defend Hungarian oilfields.

April 16, 1945: Soviets begin final attack on Berlin.

May 7, 1945: Unconditional surrender of German forces to Allies.

Hans Philipp at the controls of his Fw 190 prepares to get airborne for a sortie from Krasnogvardeisk. He had returned the first official JG 54 victory at the controls of the new fighter on December 29, 1942.

Introduction

The close of 1942 saw Germany's fortunes of war swing violently. On October 23, 1942, the much-vaunted Erwin Rommel saw the tide turn against him at the battle of El Alamein. From there, it would be eight months of non-stop retreat until the Axis forces were evicted entirely from North Africa. On the Eastern Front, in dramatic fashion, on February 2, 1943, the German 6th Army surrendered to Marshal Zhukov at Stalingrad, a defeat of epic proportion.

Jagdflieger Karl Schnörrer wrote the about the fighting in the northern sector of the Eastern Front in early 1943:

> As a fighter pilot I was starting to get the unpleasant feeling that the aerial supremacy we enjoyed would soon be a thing of the past. Everywhere you looked when flying over Russian lines there were unbroken columns of reinforcements and war matériel rolling toward the front lines. Because of the constant heavy enemy aerial activity over the Ilmensee–Staraja Russa sector, our Gruppe shifted southward to Rehilbizi. We flew daily Stuka escort sorties, always tangling with large groups of

An unusually camouflaged 2./JG 26 Fw 190 at Dno.

Leading fighter ace of the Tagjagd, Gruppenkommandeur (GKr.) I./JG 52 Erich Hartmann seen after his 350th victory.

Russian fighters as we strove to clear the skies teeming with enemy aircraft.

Not even the spectacular but doomed German offensive at Kursk—Operation *Citadel*—that July could stop the Soviet juggernaut which took less than two years to reach the steps of Reich Chancellery in Berlin.

In the West, Allied landings at Sicily in July 1943, Italy in January 1944, and Normandy in June 1944, saw the pincers inexorably close around the Reich. Last-gasp German offensives—the Ardennes, for example—merely delayed the inevitable, as did Allied blunders such as that at Arnhem. And all the while the Luftwaffe saw its Jagdgeschwader dispersed piecemeal, from sector to front, from the Balkans to the USSR, from the Mediterranean to the Oder Front, to France, and the Baltic, either trying to bolster the retreating ground forces, or dealing with the 1,000-*Viermot* raids of the USAAF and RAF that came wave upon wave, relentlessly, into the German heartland.

Luftwaffe aces multiplied exponentially, but died in combat in equal measure. From the early days of the war—it must be said, against less experienced opposition—a *Jagdflieger* could expect a Knight's Cross after 20 kills. By 1943, award thresholds in the East had been inflated by factors of four or more and for the most part somewhat arbitrarily. Lt. Emil Bitsch of III./JG 3 had returned over 100 victories before he received the Knight's Cross in August 1943, while Gerhard Thyben had 111 kills in December 1944 before getting his. Hartmann's score was nearly at 150 before his came through. On March 2, 1944, the Swords were awarded to Egon Mayer, Kommodore JG 2, in the West for 102 victories and to Gerhard Barkhorn in the East, for 251. Compare this to the top Allied aces: the RAF's "Pat" Pattle's 60-odd kills, Soviet Grigory Rechkalov's 65 kills, and USAAF pilot Richard Bong's 40 kills.

As the net closed across the Rhine in the west and the Oder in the east, Luftwaffe tactics became more and more desperate, with the *letzter Aufgebot*, the supreme sacrifice, being encouraged among young, fanatical German pilots. Operation *Elbe* was nothing short of a mass "suicide" sortie, with kamikaze-style pilots forced to ram enemy aircraft. Operation *Bodenplatte* launched on New Year's Day 1945 against Allied airpower in the West, saw almost 300 Luftwaffe fighters destroyed and over 200 pilots—novices and veterans alike—killed or captured, signalling the end of the Luftwaffe as an effective fighting force.

Lt. Joachim Göhre on his Black 10 of 8./JG 1. He was shot down and wounded on September 4, 1943 near Dunkirk. During the summer of 1943 8./JG 1 was at the forefront of USAAF raids over Western Europe and Germany. Göhre was killed on April 22, 1944, machine-gunned by P-51s as he hung in his parachute harness. Note the 8. Staffel emblem, a dog cocking its leg against a very British top hat decorated with the Union Jack and the Stars 'n' Bars.

At Mizil, Romania, "White Triple Chevron" is the Bf 109 G-2 Gustav flown by Kommandeur I./JG 4, Hptm. Franz Hahn.

In Profile:
The *Experten*

By 1943 long-serving Luftwaffe fighter pilots were flying and fighting on any number of different fronts. Having come up against weaker air forces during the first part of the war, the *Experten* would soon find themselves grossly outnumbered. But there were always large numbers of opponents to engage and shoot down. The emphasis continued to be on the acquisition of kills. High "scores" and high "scorers" fitted well into Third Reich concepts of German (Aryan) superiority. Successful fighter pilots in the Luftwaffe were elevated to leading positions in the fighter arm, success being measured by the number of claims filed. This individualistic approach was encouraged and fostered. While accumulating huge numbers of missions and victories, the *Experten* necessarily became very proficient indeed and even when facing difficult odds usually held the upper hand in terms of tactics, situational awareness, and perhaps even airmanship until well into 1944.

At the same time, as the war progressed, the German claim adjudication process grew ever more complex if not bureaucratic. The amount of paperwork involved for a victory credit was considerable. The pilot's own *Abschussmeldung*—victory report—usually had to be accompanied by a combat report, victory and witness statements and supporting testimony from the unit commander, which was passed up the chain of command. A claim confirmation—an *Abschussbestätigung*—could take months to be awarded. Insufficient details could result in the claim being denied or put in a pending file, sometimes for months or years. In other cases, claims could be filed for which no witness was found, the submission supported only by a superior officer's statement. Shared victories—common in the RAF and USAAF—were not a feature of the German system. Gun cameras—as used by USAAF pilots—were only gradually introduced in the Jagdwaffe and were then chiefly used to acquire film footage for the development of training and tactics. A victory credit board, or *Abschusskommission*, was established to manage all claims and credits. Unsurprisingly, the system had completely broken down by late 1944/early 1945. It is known for example that only 289 of Erich Hartmann's supposed 352 victories were in fact officially confirmed. In addition, only 307 of his claims had even been officially filed before the end of the war.

Two great JG 52 aces, Rall and Krupinski. Note both are wearing the Knight's Cross.

The USSR, 1943

On the Eastern Front, the Tagjagd gradually lost control of the situation throughout 1943. Ju 87 Stukas and other ground-attack types, including the later Schlacht variants of the Focke-Wulf Fw 190 were the most appropriate aircraft for missions above the vast steppes of the USSR. Increasing enemy pressure in the air was also causing the Germans heavier losses.

Among the aces lost early in the year in the East were 8./JG 54's Fw. Alfred Dettke (33 victories) shot down on January 5, and 7./JG 54's Fw. Josef Berchtl (27 victories) reported missing the following day. Walter Nowotny's *Kaczmarek*—wingman—Karl "Quax" Schnörrer wrote the following account about the fighting in the northern sector in early 1943:

> On one occasion Nowotny's Schwarm ran into 50–60 Russian fighters and we were quickly surrounded. Tracer trails whizzed across the sky in all directions like comets and after a 40-minute dogfight, with no victories to show for our efforts, our kites were riddled. Drenched in sweat and with gas running low, it was time to get out of there and make for home. Suddenly Nowotny's voice came over the radio, "I'm hit bad." In desperation we dove for home, our kites brushing the tops of the trees. A few moments later the field strip at Tuleblja came into view. Nowotny fired off some signal flares to warn the ground personnel of his predicament and dropped down toward the strip like a wounded eagle, touching down at 170 kph.

In the mess celebrating JG 54's 4000th victory, a milestone reached on February 19, 1943. Hptm. Philipp, seated underneath the green heart, is wearing his Oak Leaves with Swords, having just returned his 166th and 167th victories. Trautloft, left of the heart, is delivering a speech. According to Trautloft, by this stage of the conflict 99 JG 54 pilots had achieved ten or more victories; Trautloft himself had returned 55 at this time. On July 6, 1943 Trautloft was appointed as Jagdflieger Inspizient Ost, Inspector of Fighter Units on the Eastern Front.

Elements of JG 54 were dispatched to other sectors of the front during the second winter in Russia. Here a cannon-armed "gunboat" of 6. Staffel is seen at Zhitomir, Ukraine, early 1943.

Just at that instant flames erupted from his engine cowl. Nowotny could obviously feel the searing heat in the cockpit as he threw off his straps, jettisoned the sliding section of his canopy and, while the machine was rolling to a stand, jumped into the soft sand alongside the strip. The crate rolled another 30 meters and exploded, the detonation sending pieces of debris flying through the air.

During the opening Soviet offensive of 1943, an attempt was made to lift the siege of Leningrad, on January 8. The day before, I./JG 54 claimed 12 kills. The first went to the Staffelkapitän 2./JG 54 Oblt. Siegfried Graf von Matuschka, who downed a Yak-1 fighter (Graf von Matuschka was killed on April 16, 1943, final score 29). Half an hour later "Fips" Philipp, with his regular wingman, Uffz. Reinhardt, encountered two groups of LaGG-3s at low level. Philipp reported five kills and Reinhardt one. Staffelkapitän of 1./JG 54, Lt. Walter Nowotny, scored on this day, but his opponent was an obsolete Polikarpov I-16. On January 12, I./JG 54 filed 36 claims. Philipp accounted for eight enemy aircraft (six IL-2s and two I-16s), and among Otto Kittel's six victories were also two U-2 biplanes that literally disintegrated in midair on taking a burst from the Focke-Wulf's guns. Following a further seven I./JG 54 victories the following day, January 14 saw the "Green Hearts" shoot down 30 Soviet machines. Philipp brought down five to reach 152 victories. Two of the machines he defeated that day were from the Hurricane-operating 3rd Guards Fighter Aviation Regiment (GvIAP). Five kills were scored each by Oblt. Taumer and Fw. Tegtmeier. On January 16, 2./JG 54 lost two aircraft. Uffz. Helmut Brandt had to force-land on the frozen Lake Ladoga and was taken prisoner. His Black 2 was the first virtually undamaged Fw 190 to be captured by the Soviets.

A new wave of victories brought up JG 54's score to 4000 kills on February 19. JG 54 recorded 31 victories on this date (including 20 by I./JG 54), the victory reported by Fw. Otto Kittel (his 39th). Two others were credited to Hptm. Philipp (numbers 166 and 167). Philipp was a talented pilot and an aggressive dogfighter, going on to defeat a further eight such machines

As the fighting raged in Stalingrad, the great ace Hermann Graf departed JG 52 and the Eastern Front. The Knight's Cross winners of the unit pose one last time with their comrade.

(four Yak-1s and four LaGG-3s) on February 23 (victories 174–180) with total JG 54 claims amounting to 40 enemy aircraft shot down, 32 of these by the Fw 190s of I Gruppe.

In the far north, JG 5 faced extreme situations on the tundra.

In the southern sector, despite the desperate efforts of various Luftwaffe units, Stalingrad surrendered on February 2, 1943 while many crews fell in vain attempting to resupply the surrounded 6th Army. The Caucasus had to be evacuated in a hurry.

The Luftwaffe was increasingly relying on its Finnish, Romanian, Hungarian, and Slovak allies, which it had equipped with Bf 109 fighters as the resources of the Tagjagd continued to shrink inexorably. The Mediterranean siphoned off many fighters, while the high command sought to strengthen the defense of the Reich, German airspace increasingly under dire threat from the USAAF and RAF.

During 1943, the same Geschwader—JG 3, 5, 51, 52, and 54—continued to return victories in Russia. However, these units were rarely complete because Gruppen were regularly withdrawn from the front to be re-equipped or sent on R&R. Of note though was the temporary detachment in the East, during the first four months of the year—and just prior to the Russian onslaught against the "bulge" at Demyansk—of I./JG 26 from the Channel under 42-victory ace Maj. Johannes Seifert. Having received brand-new Fw 190 A-5s at Heilingenbeil, his pilots flew across to Relbitsy airfield, west of Lake Ilmen.

It is doubtful whether the move was welcomed by the pilots and ground crews—not for nothing was the German soldier "*froh wie Gott in Frankreich*"—happy as God in France. Accustomed to the comforts of France, Seifert's pilots had also developed a certain level of "intimacy" with the local French population. Their new living conditions were harsh: the thatched huts that served as quarters at least kept out the frost and snow. Combat conditions in the East were also radically different from those in the West—here they would encounter IL-2 Sturmoviks and Lend-Lease P-40s and Spitfires, operating at low altitude over a broad area with few, if any, landmarks. Was this a move to give the "Schlageter" pilots easy victories to boost their tallies on the part of their former CO and now General der Jagdflieger Galland? The achievement of aerial victories was still after all one of the main goals of the Jagdwaffe. Ultimately the transfer proved to be a real test of the skills and endurance of I./JG 26 pilots. Staffelkapitän (Staka) of 1./JG 26 was Hptm. Walter Hoeckner, a veteran of Crete

I./JG 26 operated for a few months in the East. Lt. Hans-Georg Dippel of 2./JG 26 describes a dogfight in front of his winter-camouflaged Fw 190. Dippel was killed on May 8, 1944 in the vicinity of Koblenz. At that time he led 9./JG 26 and was credited with 21 victories.

"It was on Lake Ladoga"

by Major Hans Philipp

For days now the storm has been howling around our barracks. Rivulets of rainwater stream from our machines, and again and again, with our noses pressed to the windows, we stare forlornly out over our sodden dispersals somewhere on the northern front. This period of enforced inactivity, the boredom of waiting interminably for an improvement in the weather was starting to play on our nerves. Patience is something that we aviators have to learn and master over time.

A new, brighter day dawns. The heavy, low-hanging clouds have started to break up and there are patches of blue sky. A few timid rays of sunlight are already glinting on our turning propellers, falling on the fresh-faced, eager young Stuka and fighter crews, finalizing the details of a long-planned joint sortie in front of the *Gefechtsstand* [command post] operations room.

The engines are throbbing as if they are as happy as we are. Water splashes from the puddles all around. We get airborne, setting out on a heading in the direction of Lake Ladoga. The mission is an anti-shipping sortie, an attack on the Soviet convoys attempting to transport supplies and reinforcements to Leningrad across the huge lake. We soon spot them. The cargo vessels and their escorts furiously open up on us with everything they have. Bang! Bang! Bang!

Our Stukas pass overhead unperturbed, seeking out the biggest, fattest cargo vessels, while our faster combat machines look for those vessels where the antiaircraft fire is concentrated. We fighters orbit the tight formations, making sure that their work is not disturbed too soon by Soviet fighters.

Now comes the order to attack. The noses of our machines are pointed down, the Stukas roll over their wingtips. The ships loom large in the sights, the glittering surface of the water rushes up to meet us. Our machine guns start to clatter while the bombs fall away from the wings of the Stukas, wobbling in the slipstream. All around burst fountains of steam, spray and water.

Splinters and debris from the vessels that have been hit whirl through the air. The shadowy profiles of our Messerschmitt fighters flit at wavetop height across the churned-up waters of the lake toward those ships "marked for death," the tracers of the machine guns and cannon marking their passage.

A cry of hoorah comes over the radio: "Let's get at them!" And then suddenly: "Watch out, Soviet fighters above." There is a moment's silence, and then, noses pointed skyward, our machines claw for altitude, leaving a plume of smoke from the guns. We dive on the enemy fighter formation from all directions, while the Soviets describe nervous, aimless orbits. Glinting prop blades are visible, while our tracers arch toward flashes of bright blue lower surfaces. Already one Bolshevik goes spinning down to plunge into the water.

"*Richtung Heimat!*"—"Let's go home!"—comes the call. We head back to load up with more bombs. We'll be back overhead in an hour. Downing enemy fighters is not the priority today—sinking those freighters is our job, to prevent Leningrad being resupplied. The fighters return to the airfield in pairs. The Stukas returned a while ago. As we leave the scene the square-shaped parachute of a shot-down enemy aviator drifts slowly down. Wreckage and oil slicks can be seen in the water. The fighting is over ... at least for an hour.

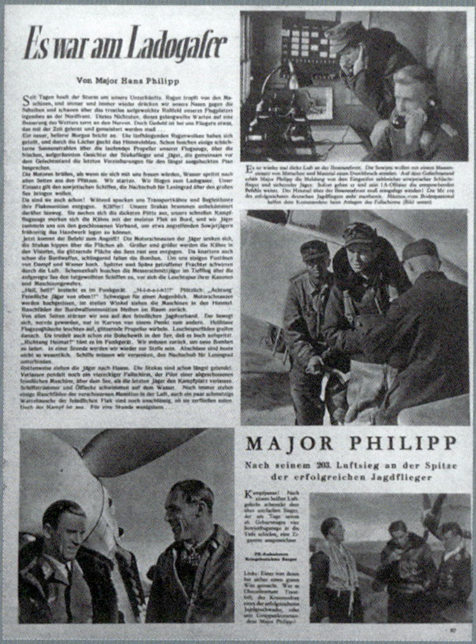
Es war am Ladogasee

Von Major Hans Philipp

MAJOR PHILIPP

Nach seinem 203. Luftsieg an der Spitze der erfolgreichen Jagdflieger

The Hans Philipp feature in *Der Adler*, April 1943.

Hptm. Wilhelm Gäth replaced Zink as Staka 2./JG 26 and is seen here in front of the same Black 8. Gäth would be wounded on January 14, 1944 near Soissons, credited with nine victories at that time.

with 6./JG 77, with 39 victories; 2./JG 26 flew under 30-victory ace Oblt. Fulbert Zink, a veteran of III./JG 53 and a former instructor at JFS 5 at Villacoublay; and 3./JG 26 were led by veteran Bf 110 *Zerstörer* pilot Hptm. Rolf Hermichen who had returned some 23 victories.

Their first action took place on February 16. I./JG 26 pilots were covering the withdrawal of ground troops from Demyansk, when they met a large formation of IL-2s; shooting down 11 for no loss, Hoeckner returned his 40th and 41st, while 1. Staffel ace Ofw. Alfred "Fred" Heckmann achieved his 54th and 55th. Heckmann left 1./JG 26 on February 28, 1943, to take up instructing duties with Ergänzung-Jagdgruppe Ost. The next day brought them down to earth. Uffz. Schnell was killed first, his Fw 190 Yellow 11 taking a direct hit from antiaircraft fire. Then Lend-Lease P-40s escorting IL-2s arrived on the scene. While fighting Yak-7s from the 28th GvIAP (239th Fighter Aviation Division, or IAD), Uffz. Kneiss in Yellow 5 crashed into the ground as he was turning at low altitude. Other pilots claimed three P-40s shot down. This was a lesson for the JG 26 pilots. Over the next three days they shot down nine Sturmoviks and one LaGG-3 with no further losses. Ensuing dogfights with Soviet fighters resulted in futher success: four shot down on February 21.

On February 23, a fierce battle took place with a group of Yak-7s from 42nd IAP, with four aircraft being shot down, identified as two LaGG-3s and two P-40s. The Yak-7s were armed with 37-mm cannon, and one German pilot took a fuselage hit from such a shell, but returned to base without problem. Two days later, four IL-2s and two LaGGs fell victim to I./JG 26 pilots. The biggest success came on March 5, when 14 Soviet aircraft fell for the loss of Fw. Karl Preeg, a new pilot who had served in the Condor Legion in Spain as a truck driver. Four of these victories were returned by Fw. Scheyd of 3./JG 26, and three by the Kommandeur himself who had only just learned the news of the death of his brother in III./JG 26, shot down and killed by Spitfires over Bailleul in the West. Two days later, the

"*Nach seinem 203 Luftsieg an der Spitze der erfolgreichen Jagdflieger*"—"following his 203rd victory, [Maj. Hans Philipp] is now the leading Luftwaffe fighter pilot," March 1943. In only 78 days, Philipp claimed no fewer than 80 kills, Appointed Kommodore of JG 1 in the West, he handed command of I./JG 54 over to Maj. Reinhard Seiler.

Asse unserer Jagdflieger

an der Eismeerfro

Alle Aufnahmen: Kriegsberichter Hirschf

Fernschreiben

+ A LYTS 403 2/5 1515 DGZ =
LW- KRIEGSBERICHTERZUG NORW.- FINNL.
LT HENKELS UEBER LFL 5, ROEM EINS C PRESSE =
JAGDFLIEGER AN DER EISMEERFRONT MIT IHREN
ABSCHUSSZAHLEN :
OFW. MUELLER 91 ABSCHUESSE.-
OBLT. EHRLER 83 ABSCHUESSE.-
LT. WEISSENBERGER 77 ABSCHUESSE.
HPTM. CARGANICO 52 ABSCHUESSE.-
FW. DOEBRICH 52 ABSCHUESSE.-
OFW. BRUNNER 46 ABSCHUESSE.-
FW. BARTELS 46 ABSCHUESSE.-
MAJOR SCHOLTZ 32 ABSCHUESSE.-
OBLT. SEGATZ 31 ABSCHUESSE.-
FW. SCHUCK 29 ABSCHUESSE.-
OBLT. TETZNER 20 ABSCHUESSE .- +

"Asse an der Eismeerfront"—Aces of the Arctic Sea front. An early 1943 press release detailing the scores of the leading aces of JG 5. Photographed around March 8, 1943, the main image features eight pilots of the leading Staffel in II./JG 5 in front of Lt. Weissenberger's Yellow 4. Six of these eight 6./JG 5 pilots either had been or would be awarded the Knight's Cross.

Staka of 1./JG 26, Hptm. Hoeckner, displayed virtuoso shooting skills, bringing down five Sturmoviks and one P-40. Other pilots achieved only three victories on that day.

With the successful evacuation from the Demyansk Pocket in April, Seifert's pilots had scored 75 victories, and were now moved south, to Shalatovka near Smolensk, where the unit supported the last stage of the evacuation of German troops from the wedge in the Rzhev–Vyazma area. Combat activity dropped so low that 3./JG 26 was assigned to fighting partisans. Using pilots experienced in fighting heavy bombers to fight these kinds of combatants was clearly a waste of resources. Therefore, I./JG 26 returned to France at the beginning of June, having scored 127 victories in the East—17 of these achieved by Hptm. Hoeckner, 11 by Johannes Seifert, and nine by Fw. Willius. Casualties were eight pilots, including the Staka of 2./JG 26, Hptm. Zink, who failed to return from a free hunt over Staraja-Russa on March 14, 1943 after giving chase to a Pe-2 well behind enemy lines.

Elsewhere on the northern front, the Kommandeur I./JG 54, Maj. Hans Philipp—on his 26th birthday, March 17, 1943—claimed four more Soviet aircraft shot down, which took his total to 203. This made him the highest-scoring fighter pilot in the Luftwaffe. While JG 52's Hermann Graf was the first to reach the 200-mark on October 2, 1942, he had immediately been taken off operations and had not returned any victories subsequently.

During 1943 no fewer than five awards of the Oak Leaves to the Knight's Cross were issued to pilots fighting in the East: on January 11, Oblt. Gerhard Barkhorn (4./JG 52) was awarded the Oak Leaves for 105 victories; on August 2, two JG 5 pilots, Hptm. Erich Ehrler and Oblt. Theodor Weissenberger, received the award for their 112 victories each; on November 25, Obstlt. Dietrich Hrabak, Kommodore of JG 54, was also awarded the Oak Leaves for 118 victories.

On September 12, the Swords to the Knight's Cross were allocated to Hptm. Günther Rall (leading III./JG 52) for his 200 *Abschüsse*. On October 29, the Knight's Cross was awarded to Lt. Erich Hartmann leading 9./JG 52 for his 148 *Abschüsse*. He would go on to become the greatest ace in the history of aviation.

While there was undeniable quality within the Tagjagd, from a quantitative point of view, the Luftwaffe was totally swamped in the East. During the first half of the year, 13 Knight's Cross bearers were lost: leading 10./JG 51, Oblt. Wolfgang Böwing-Treuding's Fw 190 was hit by antiaircraft fire during a strafing attack on a column near Dubnitza on February 11. He was awarded the Knight's Cross posthumously for his 46 victories in the East (including 15

Hptm. Günther Rall (III./JG 52), seen here at Nikolajew, received the Swords in September 1943.

Fw. Hans Döbrich's Bf 109 G-2 Yellow 10 (W.Nr. 13916), an MG 151/20 *Gondelwaffen* cannon-toting "gun-boat." Another 6./JG 5 ace, Döbrich returned his 50th victory on March 23, 1943 during yet another *Freiejagd* "free-hunt" sortie over the Murmansk region, downing two P-40s. Note the II.Gruppe four-leaf clover on the cowl and the short-lived 6. Staffel badge visible below the cockpit, a *Mickey Maus* ripping the tail off a Soviet aircraft.

IL-2s). Ground fire also brought down Oblt. Gustav Denk, leading 6./JG 52. On February 13, he had just destroyed two aircraft on the ground at an aerodrome when his Bf 109 G exploded in midair. He likewise received the Knight's Cross posthumously for his 67 victories (two in the West). Austrian Lt. Karl Hammerl began flying in his country's air force before the Anschluss. Posted to 1./JG 52, he had been awarded the Knight's Cross on September 19, 1942 for his 55 *Luftsiege*. On March 2, 1943, with 67 victories, he crash-landed behind enemy lines southwest of Kolomak. He died in a Soviet PoW camp.

On April 10, 1943 Ofw. Willi Nemitz of 6./JG 52 was killed in combat with Soviet fighters. Flying out of Anapa in the Caucasus, eyewitnesses saw his Bf 109 G-4 Yellow 3 (W.Nr. 14898) plunge earthward out of the cloud deck north of Nishne-Bakanskaja and bury itself deep in the ground. Aged 32, Willi "Altvater" (grandfather) Nemitz was one of the oldest operational fighter pilots in the Jagdwaffe. One of the old guard of JG 52, he joined II. Gruppe during the Battle of Britain but did not claim his first victory until he started operations in the East, downing a DB-3 bomber on July 3, 1941. Although an Oberfeldwebel, a flight sergeant, he was appointed Staffelkapitän of 6./JG 52 on March 11, 1943 in recognition of his excellent leadership and fighter pilot skills. Willi Nemitz was credited with 81 victories in around 500 missions, and posthumously promoted to the rank of Leutnant.

On April 19, Obfw. Rudolf Müller, one of the great aces of JG 5 in the far north (94 victories) was forced to land on a frozen lake. He tried to regain his lines but, after several days, was intercepted by a patrol of Red Army skiers. Mystery surrounds his disappearance,

6./JG 5 was the undisputed *Experten-Staffel* of the far north and Ofw. "Rudi" Müller (right) was its first big ace. His 92nd victory on March 13, 1943 was the 500th for 6. Staffel. Knight's Cross holders Weissenberger and Staka Ehrler complete the line-up. Müller was posted missing on April 19, 1943. He was the leading ace of JG 5 at the time of his capture, with 94 kills.

but it would appear that he died in a Soviet PoW camp. Another JG 5 ace perished the following month: Albert Brunner had been credited with around 50 victories and was awarded a posthumous Knight's Cross.

Oak Leaves bearers were not spared either: on February 21, "Assi" Hahn, Kommandeur II./JG 54, was shot down south of Salutsche after clashing with Soviet fighters. Hahn had voluntarily requested his transfer from III./JG 2 because, for him, the fate of the war was being decided in the East. He was held in captivity for seven years. Hahn had attained 108 *Luftsiege*. On March 6, Oblt. Hans Beisswenger, Kapitän of 6./JG 54, was engaged in combat with a large number of LaGG 3 fighters. He apparently downed two before he was hit in the engine. His wingman, Uffz. Georg Munderloh, radioed that he and Beisswenger were attempting to return to their lines at low altitude but both were reported missing. Beisswenger had 152 victories to his credit (one in the West), including 32 since the turn of the year, while Munderloh had downed 20 during the same period.

In July, the Wehrmacht launched a major counteroffensive in the Kursk salient. With little headway being made against Russian defenses, the operation was soon curtailed, interrupted as a result of the Italian volte-face. The impact of *Zitadelle* (*Citadel*) would be significant because, as one author wrote, "If Stalingrad proved that Germany could not win the war in the east, Kursk was proof that it could also lose it."

On July 6, Major Reinhard Seiler (109 victories, including nine in Spain), leading I./JG 54, was shot and seriously wounded. Declared unfit for operations, he was posted to a training school. On July 8, Obfw. Hubert Strassl (8./JG 51) was shot down near Kursk in a dogfight with LaGG-3s. He jumped clear but his parachute failed to deploy. He received the Knight's Cross posthumously for his 67 victories in the East. The next day, July 9, four aircraft from 7./JG 52 flew a reconnaissance sortie toward Belgorod. Seeing one of his comrades making an emergency landing, Obfw. Edmund Rossmann (93 victories and a Knight's Cross bearer) also put down close by to pick him up in his 109. But Soviet soldiers rapidly appeared on the scene and Rossmann was taken captive, spending six years in Po W camps. On July 26, 1943, Lt. Josef Jennewein of I./JG 51 disappeared near Orel. An Austrian, he was an expert skier who had won several competitions. Holder of 86 victories (five in the West), "Pepi" Jennewein was awarded the Knight's Cross posthumously.

Another ace lost was the recently appointed Kommandeur of I./JG 54, Maj. Gerhard Homuth.

"Assi" Hahn (left), voluntarily departed JG 2 for the Eastern Front. The new Kommandeur II./JG 54 is seen here with Oblt. Max Stotz (middle) and Hans "Beisser" Beisswenger (killed March 6, 152 victories). These three "100+" aces are celebrating Hahn's 100th and Stotz's 150th; each had been in action since the start of the war. Stotz was a pre-war Austrian Air Force pilot and had returned his first kill on November 7, 1939. Note the portraits on the wall: Göring and Galland.

One of the B-24s downed during *Tidal Wave*. August 1, 1943.

In Profile:

Romania: I./JG 4 against the USAAF

Romanian oilfields, essential for the Wehrmacht war effort, had already been the target of Soviet bombers in June 1941. In 1942, the *Halpro* mission had shown that the USAAF was also interested in this strategic sector. To counter this potential threat, I./JG 4 was established on July 31, 1942 with veterans from the East, primarily from JG 77, and new, young pilots. The Gruppe was led by Hptm. Franz Hahn, ex-Kapitän of 11./JG 51, and was based between Mizil and Mamaia, covering a large area. Ofw. Reinhold Schmetzer and Fw. Albert Palm, with 33 and 28 victories respectively, were posted in from 8./JG 77.

On August 1, 1943, with bases in Libya (Benghazi), a large B-24 formation took off to attack several Romanian refineries as part of an ambitious operation codenamed *Tidal Wave*. Over Romania, the Liberators faced heavy antiaircraft defenses, the Romanian Air Force, and I./JG 4. A large number of B-24s were downed. Hptm. Hans Eder, Adjutant of I./JG 4, related his part of the battle in a letter home:

> We immediately dove for the deck and caught their formation unawares at an altitude of 200 meters. We had to take care to pull up to avoid smashing into the ground before closing in to mount our attack. I was able to level out alongside two of these "furniture vans" as they plowed through the skies. They both immediately opened up on me. Not wishing to hang around, I pulled up my mount and banked over to come around in behind one of them. I first eliminated the tail gunner with his twin cannon. My salvos then ripped into an engine, which exploded. A large sheet flame erupted from the bomber's fuselage, enveloping the aircraft, which fell away and smashed into the ground moments later with its crew of seven still onboard. It was a very successful baptism of fire.

Tidal Wave was a disaster for the attackers—of the 165 B-24s that took part in the attack, 52 were lost. On the following day—August 2—only 33 bombers out of the 178 in action the previous day were airworthy. The Americans lost 879 men killed, missing, or taken prisoner. But despite a loss rate approaching some 40 percent, *Tidal Wave* was the first of a series of actions over Romania that would grow in intensity the following year.

Fw. Albert Palm, a 28-victory ace with 8./JG 77, was posted to the newly established I./JG 4 at Mizil, northeast of Ploesti, Romania.

The late H-J. Marseille's strict superior had departed Africa, a victim of malaria, and then temporarily held a position in Sofia. He voluntarily returned to the front but was reported missing on August 2, 1943, in combat with P-39Airacobras on one of his first flights in the East. He was credited with 63 *Abschüsse*. Günther Josten—assigned at the end of August 1942 to 3./JG 51 on the Eastern Front—began his long run of kills during the Kursk offensive. On July 10, 1943 he made claims 8–10. Three days later, on July 13, he shot down five IL-2 Sturmoviks for victories 12–16. In total he claimed 19 victories in July and 30 in August 1943 to begin a remarkable series that saw him achieve some 178 victories over 420 sorties without ever being shot down. The war ended for Josten as Gruppenkommandeur of IV./JG 51—his last seven aerial victories being claimed on April 25, 1945. His brother, Reinhard Josten, also served in Jagdgeschwader 51 and was killed in action on April 25, 1942. Günther Josten described some of his experiences in his memoir *Gefechtsbericht*:

> July 8, 1943. Oskar brought down several Russians on the early morning sortie flown with the boss. I had the same luck as yesterday—playing "hide-and-seek" with eight LaGGs in the cloud deck. Sometimes they'd stick their noses out from their cover but when I tried a firing pass, they'd quickly pop back in again. I blazed away but it drove me crazy. Nothing doing—no luck whatsoever. All the others got IL-2s or fighters which they were able to bring down without so much as a dogfight! It makes me sick!! I flew the last sortie of the day with Lt. Höfemeier *ohne Feindberührung*—no contact with the enemy. We flew low over the battlefield and could observe the fighting that was raging … huge numbers of tanks slugging it out as if in a giant arena. As the light was fading, we could see every strike on target quite clearly. On the horizon batteries of Stalin organs [rocket launchers] could be seen unleashing salvo after salvo. Super to watch—*ganz toll* … well done.
>
> 9 July: I'm woken again early by aircraft low over the field waggling their wings! A lot of victories again. Well, my turn tomorrow, I'm flying the early sortie in the morning … as it is I fly the second mission of the day. As soon as we get airborne, we hear that there's a lot of aggro going on over the southern sector but by the time we get there, there's nothing to see. Not a single Russian. At this rate I shall soon depair. At midday I'm up again with Oskar and he manages two Zement bombers. I could p …. ! but I'm happy enough anyway as Lt. Brendel manages his 50th and we have now achieved 400 in the Staffel with the kill returned by Ofw. Kossatz. This afternoon I was up again, this time flying with the boss and hoping to have more luck with him … we spot six MiG-3s but no sooner have they sighted us than they hightail it for home.

Oblt. Joachim Brendel was the long-time Staffelkapitän of 1./JG 51.

Aces of 1./JG 54—the other three members of the so-called "Nowotny Schwarm." From left: Fw. Anton Döbele, 94 victories in 458 sorties; Uffz. Karl "Quax" Schnörrer, long-time wingman of Nowotny, Knight's Cross on March 22, 1945 for 46 victories including 11 flying the Me 262; and Rudolf Rademacher, Knight's Cross on September 30, 1944, 97 victories and who flew the Me 262 with 11./JG 7 from January 1945, returning 16 victories on *Turbos*.

> At 20:15 Fw. Moritz Franke's *Ferntrauung* [marriage by proxy]. The Kommodore is with us for the rest of the evening's festivities. Moritz and Piepel are awarded the Iron Class 2nd class and the combat clasp in bronze. I get the silver combat clasp for 60 sorties. Well, a bit of a consolation prize for my run of bad luck, you could say.

On July 9, Oblt. Joachim Brendel of 1./JG 51 flying his Fw 190 A-6 White 1 scored his 50th victory in the region of Orel. He would not be awarded his Knight's Cross until his 100th. He achieved his 150th on October 16, 1944, earning himself the Oak Leaves. On January 14, 1945 his score stood at 156. At that stage of the war he had been promoted to Hauptmann and was Gruppenkommandeur of III./JG 51. His final victory came on April 25, 1945—despite the odds he returned 40 victories during 1945, including four on February 18 and a further four on February 21, including three IL-2s. He finished the war with 189 victories and emerged as JG 51's highest scorer on the Eastern Front.

On September 1, 1943, the Kommandeur of II./JG 52, Hptm. Helmut Kühle, left the Gruppe for an attaché posting in Sofia, Bulgaria. His successor was Hptm. Gerhard Barkhorn, who would hold this position until shot down and badly injured in May 1944. Exactly one week after his appointment Barkhorn flew two missions, the first in the early morning when he scrambled and shot down an IL-2 and an La-5. That afternoon he dispatched another La-5 fighter at 14:35. Upon his return to Karlofka, he was congratulated for his new total of 172 *Abschüsse* by his chief mechanic Uffz. Kustere. During that month Barkhorn´s II. Gruppe claimed a total of 109 VVS (Soviet Air Forces) aircraft over Kharkov, Belgorod, and Senkov, losing just two Bf 109 G-6s in air combat. Of these the most notable loss was the Staffelkapitan of 6./JG 52, Oblt. Heinz Schmidt. On September 5, after shooting down an La-5 and an IL-2 within five minutes, for his 172nd and 173rd *Abschüsse*, Schmidt disappeared in his Yellow 7 and was never seen again.

JG 54, Nowotny on his White 8 celebrating 300 victories for 1. Staffel.

During the summer and autumn of 1943, Walter Nowotny was a veritable one-man air force in the skies over the Eastern Front. The young Austrian pilot was already a Knight's Cross bearer. In June, as Staka 1./JG 54, he claimed 41 aircraft shot down for the month—on June 15 he reached 100 victories, while nine days later, on downing ten enemy aircraft, he increased his total to 124 kills.

When Nowotny became Kommandeur of I./JG 54 on August 21, 1943, his score was 127 victories. During that month his total rose by 49—including nine on the 13th and seven on the 21st—and he reported a further 45 in September with ten on September 1 alone. In a letter home he wrote:

> Yesterday [21 August]. I achieved my 161st aerial victory. I have shot down 37 enemy aircraft in the last ten days. Max Stotz now has 186 but I'm getting damned close to him. Yesterday I downed seven and was named Kommandeur; two happy events that were celebrated in due style. Its not every day a 22-year-old Oberleutnant is appointed Kommandeur, a post normally held by a Major which means that sooner or later I will be promoted to Hauptmann and then maybe even made up to the rank of Major. But I'm not going to start dreaming about that. I still haven't been awarded the Oak Leaves.

On September 8 he passed 200 victories and was promoted to Hauptmann, while two weeks later he received the Swords to his Knight's Cross with Oak Leaves. He brought down 32 Soviet aircraft in the first two weeks of October, and on the 14th he became the first Luftwaffe pilot to achieve 250 victories. One of these, scored on the October 9, was the 6,000th to be achieved by the "Green Hearts."

Lt. Emil "Bully" Lang, ex-Lufthansa *Flugkapitän*, at the controls of his Fw 190. Lang was appointed Staffelkapitän 5./JG 54 after Staka Stotz was reported missing on August 19, 1943. During October and November 1943 Lang progressed his score from 24 to 125 victories.

Oblt. "Max" Stotz returned some 182 victories officially confirmed, including eight in the West, seen here with his rudder scoreboard displaying 100 victories, for which he was awarded the Oak Leaves on October 30, 1942. He was posted missing near Vitebsk on August 19, 1943.

On 19 October, he became the eighth recipient of the Diamonds—*Brillanten*. The Nazi propaganda machine turned Nowotny into a star. He had received the highest military awards available and was withdrawn from combat. During the following months, his main role was to perform propaganda and morale-boosting duties. On April 1, 1944, Hptm. Nowotny was appointed Kommodore of JG 101, an operational fighter training unit based at Pau in France.

On November 22, 1943 the Knight's Cross was awarded to two more "Grünherz" pilots: Lt. Emil Lang, a civilian instructor at Lufthansa, had started the war on transports. He had only joined the Jagdwaffe in 1943 as a 34-year-old, an advanced age for a *Tagjäger*. He won his first victory in March 1943 in 1./JG 54 and progressed his score to 119 kills eight months later. Obfw. Albin Wolf had joined 6./JG 54 in May 1942 and received the Knight's Cross after 117 *Luftsiege*. Both were later awarded the Oak Leaves and both were killed in 1944. As can be seen, the Knight's Cross, initially requiring 20 victories, was becoming more and more difficult to obtain. On December 11, 1943 another JG 51 ace was reported missing—Fw. Rudolf Wagner had arrived in 10./JG 51 in early 1942 and flew as Otto Gaiser's wingman. He recorded most of his victories during the summer and fall of 1943 and was credited with 81 kills at the time he went missing. His Knight's Cross was awarded posthumously on March 26, 1944.

Funeral ceremony for Ofw. Anton Döbele, killed in action on November 11, 1943 after colliding with an IL-2 and crashing in Fw 190 White 11. His Knight's Cross was awarded posthumously with a promotion to Leutnant. The guard of honor comprises, from left: Kittel, Rademacher, von Bonin, Tegtmeier and Schnörrer.

Bf 109 G-4, flown by the Gruppenkommandeur II./JG 26, Hptm. Karl-Heinz "Conny" Meyer, being refuelled at Abbeville-Drucat late December 1942/early January 1943. II./JG 26 flew a number of Bf 109 G-4 Gustavs equipped with the gondola weapons systems which were deployed alongside the unit's Fw 190s. In January 1943 Meyer was posted to a training school and from June 18, 1943 to 14 April 14, 1944 he served as GKr. 104. His successor as GKr. II./JG 26 was Maj. Wilhelm-Ferdinand Galland.

The West and the Reich, 1943

In early 1943 USAAF bomber formations started to venture into northwest Germany targeting U-boat bases at Wilhelmshaven, Emden, and Kiel, among the first German cities to experience carpet bombing. At the Casablanca conference (January 14), the Western Allies, harassed by Stalin, agreed to embark upon a continuous bombing offensive against German industries: by day the USAAF Flying Fortresses; by night the RAF Lancasters.

Two leading aces of JG 26 in the West: at right is GKr. II./JG 26 Major Wilhelm-Ferdinand "Wutz" Galland, one of the four Galland brothers. In the cockpit is JG 26 ace Joachim Müncheberg. They both fell in combat during 1943.

The tall Major Anton Mader, Kommodore of JG 11 seen in discussion with his men at Jever. Kommandeur II./JG 11 was Günther Specht, who, although losing an eye in 1939, continued to fly operations.

To reach northern Germany the American formations had to cross the Netherlands and Belgium, sectors that had seen a reduction in defensive day fighter cover. JG 1 would be increasingly called into action and an in-depth reorganization became necessary. On April 1, 1943, JG 1 received a new Kommodore in the person of veteran Hans Philipp. In the Reich itself, JG 11 was created in April 1943 by the simple expedient of splitting JG 1 into two. Maj. Anton Mader was appointed Geschwaderkommodore. Mader was born on January 7, 1913 in Castelnuovo in the Dalmatian territory of Austro-Hungary. After the Anschluss, he joined the Luftwaffe. At the outbreak of war he was commanding 3./JG 76 and then served on the staff of JG 2 and I./JG 2. In June 1941 he took up the post of Kommandeur II./JG 77, fighting at the head of his unit in Russia and Africa. He was awarded the Knight's Cross after scoring 40 victories.

German fighters had to develop a variety of new tactics to counter the enormous firepower of the Flying Fortresses. Each U.S. bomber combat "box"—combining three 18-airplane groups stacked at lower, medium, and high levels—bristled with .50-caliber machine guns firing 14 rounds a second with an effective range of 400 meters. The two-ounce bullets remained lethal against a human body at ranges of up to four miles. A B-17 formation, dubbed a "*Pulk*" (herd) by the Germans, was an unnerving sight for a fighter pilot. With a combined closing speed of 500 mph (800 kph) both sides had only seconds to make their shots count. Barreling in at 250 meters per second a fighter pilot might have time for only a half-second burst before having to take evasive action. While many of the great aces—even when outnumbered—could handle themselves with ease in the East, the air war in the West was a different kettle of fish. "Fips" Phillips, with over 200 Eastern Front victories, noted while in command of JG 1 defending against American bombers over northern Germany:

Hptm. "Toni" Hackl was appointed Kommandeur of III./JG 11. Here he is wearing the Oak Leaves, awarded in August 1942 for his long run of success in the East with JG 77. His last victory on this front was achieved on September 19, his 118th.

> Against 20 Russians trying to shoot you down or even 20 Spitfires, it can be exciting, even fun. You just had to stay alert. But curve in towards a formation of 40 Fortresses and all your past sins flash before your eyes. When you think what you are up against, it's so overwhelming that it is hard to inspire your men.

In Western Europe, it would prove increasingly difficult to get close to the four-engined *Viermots* as British or American fighter escorts often kept the attackers at a distance. Over the Reich, where the escort could not operate, the frontal attack was preferred. Closing at a speed of 400–500 kph, the Fw 190 and Bf 109s had to fly through curtains of fire created by the hundreds of machine-gunners of the B-17 or B-24s.

On April 17, 1943, pilots of the newly formed JG 11 took off to oppose a raid by four-engined USAAF bombers for the first time. The Americans were headed for Bremen. During this sortie, JG 11 returned some 11 victories and two HSS. II./ JG 11 flew another defensive sortie on May 14, 1943 from Jever. Once again 250-kg bombs were loaded onto the belly racks of 5. Staffel Bf 109 Gustavs. It was Knoke who came up with the rather radical idea of dropping bombs on the bomber formations. The theory was that a Bf 109 would ascend to an altitude of 9,000 meters, positioning over a group of bombers and release a time-fused bomb set to explode with 15 seconds' delay. A bomb detonating between American bombers flying in close formation would, it was hoped, tear the tightly packed *Pulk* apart. This method was employed for the first time on March 22, 1943, when a bomb dropped by Oblt. Knoke accounted for one Flying Fortress and damaged two others. That morning a U.S. bomber formation comprising some 136 B-17s and B-24s headed for the shipyards at Kiel. Knoke and his 5./JG 11 were airborne at 11:30. Knoke recalled:

> we were airborne with bombs against an American formation heading for Kiel. Over Holstein we tried several times to set up for an attack in tight formation but just as we were in position to release our bombs, the Americans swung into a

Staffelkapitän 9./JG 2 Oblt. Siegfried Schnell's elaborately decorated Fw 190 A-4 (W.Nr. 746) displaying 75 victories on the rudder, his tally when he handed over command to "Sepp" Wurmheller in early April 1943.

Knoke, appointed Kapitän of 5. Staffel on May 1, 1943, is seen here with his Staffel in front of Black 1, Bf 109 G-6 (W.Nr. 2008), Jever, June 1943. From left: Uffz. Helmut Lennartz, Fw. Hans Raddatz, Fw. Hans-Gerd Wennekers, Lt. Andreas Trockels, Knoke, Staffelkapitän, Lt. Kilian, Obgefr. Peter Reinhard, Fw. Erich Fürhrmann, Ofw. Leo-Lothar Barann, and Uffz. Herbert Biermann.

turn, evidently having worked out what our intention actually was. Over Kiel itself we then came under heavy antiaircraft fire from the naval base and their fire was pretty accurate which considerably disrupted our plans. As we took evasive action, I could see the Yankees release their bombs over the Germania shipyard—they were fantastically accurate. I gave the order, "Attack separately" but my bomb failed to detonate. I had to fall back on my onboard armament and dove in for a frontal attack on a group of about 30 Fortresses flying slightly apart from the others. Almost immediately I felt hits in the fuselage of my Gustav and broke off. The engine was still running like clockwork. A quick glance at the instruments showed no untoward indications. I decided to fly another frontal pass and closed on the formation again. My first burst slammed into the cockpit of a Boeing—it reared up like a wounded animal and then went down whirling into a tight right-hand spiral. At 3,000 meters above the ground it started to break up, one of its wings sheared off. At 12:17 the Fortress smashed into the ground near Husum. I headed for home, having taken several more hits in the fuselage and rudder.

On June 20, 1943, there was a change in command at I./JG 11. Hptm. Erwin Clausen, born on August 5, 1911 in Berlin, was appointed Kommandeur.

Lt. Heinz Knoke in late April 1943, at Jever, standing by the tail of Bf 109 G-1 (W.Nr. 14049) Black 3 flown by 5./JG 11 pilot Fw. Hans-Gerd Wennekers.

Clausen began his career in the navy and in 1935 moved to the Luftwaffe. In September 1939, with the rank of Feldwebel, he scored his first air victory over Poland with I./LG 2. During *Barbarossa* he commanded 1./JG 77, and from July, 1942 he was Staffelkapitan of 6./JG 77. In July he tallied some 45 victories within three weeks. Because of his distinctive facial profile, he was nicknamed "Caesar." As an Oberleutnant, having scored 52 victories, he was awarded the Knight's Cross on May 19, 1942. On July 23, 1942, he was awarded the Oak Leaves to his Knight's Cross on the occasion of his 101st victory.

By scraping the bottom of the barrel, the Luftwaffe command managed to transfer some meager reinforcements to the defense of the Reich: I./JG 27 from the Mediterranean and III./JG 54 from the East. III./JG 3, led by 51-victory ace, Kommandeur Hptm. Walther Dahl, also arrived from Russia and settled in at Münster-Handorf on the western German border. Subordinated to Jagdfliegerführer (JaFü) Holland at Deelen with instructions to be combat ready as soon as possible, the Gruppe gave up their Bf 109 G-4s and took on charge new Bf 109 G-6 "Gustavs." The Gustavs were fitted with the underwing Rüstsatz VI gondola cannon kits—the so-called *Gondelwaffen* consisting of two 2-cm Mauser MG 151/20 underwing gunpods with 135 rpg in an attempt to turn the Bf 109 into dedicated "bomber killers."

While 8. and 9. Staffeln deployed large-caliber cannon, 7. Staffel—the so-called *Kometen Staffel* (Comet Staffel)—flew machines toting WGr. 21 rocket launchers. The Werfegranate was a 21-cm-diameter air-to-air rocket with a time fuse, designed to be lobbed into the *Pulks* from a safe distance—Heinz Knoke mentions a figure of 2,000 feet in his memoir—to break up flying cohesion and the integrity of the formation, thus exposing individual B-17s to fighter attack. As a weapon it was never intended to be a pinpoint application as was the case with Allied air-launched rockets. The launch tubes—"stovepipes"—were angled at 15 degrees due to the considerable drop of these projectiles after the short rocket-burn time. The rockets were equipped with time-delayed fuses (around 15 seconds) and were known as rocket mortars due to the mortar-like trajectory. After an attack the rocket tubes could

When I./JG 26 departed for the East at the beginning of 1943, III./JG 54 replaced the Gruppe in the West. In May, on takeoff from Wevelgem, Lt. Erwin Leykauf of the Stab III./JG 54 was forced to crash-land but was unharmed. He would end the war flying Me 262 jets and returned 33 victories.

be jettisoned in case of enemy fighter threats because of the negative impact on the aircraft aerodynamics.

Losses were mounting among the young and increasingly briefly trained German pilots but also among the veterans. Hptm. Friedrich Geisshardt had won his first victory in Poland in 1939. After hard fighting with I./JG 77 (USSR and Malta), he left Africa to take over III./JG 26. On April 5, 1943, fatally wounded in combat with B-17s over Belgium, he managed to carry out an emergency landing but died the next day at the *Lazarett* (field hospital) in Ghent.

On May 15, III. /JG 54, recalled from the East, led one of its first battles against *Viermots* near Helgoland Island off the coast of northern Germany. Hptm. Günther Fink, leading 8./JG 54, was shot down over the sea during a pass through a B-17 formation. Holder of the Knight's Cross, he had 46 victories to his credit, nine won at night on the Leningrad front.

On July 17, 1943, some 332 U.S. bombers attacked Hamburg and Hanover. Five Messerschmitt Bf 109 "Toni" T-2s of Jasta Helgoland joined JG 11 in mounting defensive sorties. Uffz. Erich Ulmschneider was one of the Jasta pilots airborne that day:

> We already had a hunch that things were going to get unpleasant from early that morning, having heard the radio announce, "Strong enemy concentrations forming up over southern England." At around 10.40 cockpit readiness was ordered and we were scrambled at 11.00. Airborne with five Tonis, one Rotte of two machines led by Lt. Hondt, with me as a *Katschmarek* [wingman] and a Kette of three led by Fw. Erich Carius, we headed out on course 320 degrees. The Amis were flying a northern route from Helgoland to Wilhelmshaven. Having reached an altitude of 6,000 meters, we spotted a group of 20–25 B-17s and headed toward them. We drew alongside them, maintaining a distance of 1,500 meters and then overtook them to be able to turn back into position for a frontal attack. As we could fly no faster than 420 kph, it took us a long time to pull some 3 kilometers ahead of the bomber formation. After sweeping around in a banked curve to port, Lt. Hondt closed on the bombers head-on at full throttle, while Fw. Carius and two other machines were still trying to take up a convenient position for an attack. So there were only two of us to attack some 30 Boeings. They were able to concentrate their defensive fire on us beautifully. I was overcome with a sort of "hunting fever" as I had already eased a B-17 into my gunsight, and we were still 1,000 meters away from each other. Time to open fire. I fired a burst from my MGs and was about to squeeze the firing button of my two wing-mounted cannon when something exploded very close by me. I felt enormous air pressure pinning me back into my seat; I could no longer see a thing. While running in for the attack I had pushed up my goggles, protection against shrapnel, to get a better view. The Amis had hit my reinforced glass windshield and numerous splinters of glass had lashed into my face. I was expecting to collide with the bombers, but nothing happened. I managed to see out of the corner of one eye and concluded that the tracers had zipped past me from the rear, hence almost certainly saving me from colliding with the Amis! When my tears cleared my vision a little, I glanced all around … no sign of either Boeings or my comrades. So, I turned onto a southerly course, which would bring me over the North Sea coastline. The engine was running smoothly and I was able to calm myself down a little myself. This is how my first encounter with a Boeing ended—a life-or-death experience.

In Profile:
Lt. Eberhard Burath

In October 1942, on completion of his fighter pilot training and aged 24, Eberhard Burath was posted to JG 1 and would remain with this unit until March 1944. He would claim six *Viermots* shot down during this period. He was initially assigned to 11./JG 1, based at Mönchengladbach. By February 1943, Burath was fulfilling the role of Gruppenadjutant in I./JG 1. On May 21, 1943, I./JG 1 was scrambled twice against USAAF four-engined bombers. Up from Deelen the Fw 190s were unable to locate the incoming bombers and put down at Schipol. They were airborne again as the bombers returned from their targets in northern Germany. Burath later recalled:

> at 12:21 we were scrambled again against the bombers as they headed home. This time we were correctly vectored onto them. At around 100 km north of Ameland we ran into their formation as they were headed in a northwesterly direction for home. I was flying as Rottenflieger to Hptm. Schnoor. We overtook the bombers and turned into them to set up a head-on pass. I was too low and from this difficult angle could only bring fire to bear on the right outer B-17. I held on for three long seconds, letting him have it from all barrels—with no visible effect. On landing I must have looked more than a little surprised as Hptm. Schnoor congratulated me on my first victory! But I had other matters on my mind. As we had broken off from the enemy formation, I had seen an Fw 190 plunge into the sea and then a parachute pop open overhead. I had set my stopwatch and flew back on a reciprocal course and noted where I had overflown the coast. Oblt. Munz was missing, my old roommate from Mönchengladbach. I was determined to look for him and, when my aircraft had been made ready, took off again a short while later on my own. Heading out over the coast I started the stopwatch and quartered the sea left and right when I arrived over the area. I soon caught sight of a yellow object on the waves—a dinghy being tossed about on the stormy waves! To my angry disappointment I saw that it was empty. I orbited overhead in tight circles. "Hans, *Mensch*, where are you?" Nothing. The red low-fuel-level warning lamp flashed on: 68 minutes. An air-sea rescue plane had been sent out. I returned to refuel and then rendezvoused back out over the sea with the Seenot Wal. This time, 73 minutes. By now it was getting dark and soon the air-sea rescue craft had to break off its search. The loss of Munz affected me deeply—had he seen us searching for him? And what must have been his despair as we turned back for home? Six weeks later his body was found washed up on the beach at Sylt. A better friend I never knew.

On July 26, Burath participated in an attack on USAAF B-17s in the Leeuwarden area. In the ensuing battle, Burath's Fw 190 was hit and he was forced to carry out a belly-landing in a potato field near Buitenpost. He was shot down again on February 10, 1944 while attacking USAAF B-17s over Braunschweig. He successfully bailed out, landing near Watenstedt uninjured. On March 1, 1944, Oblt. Burath was appointed Staffelkapitän of 4./JG 1 but was shot down again on March 29, 1944.

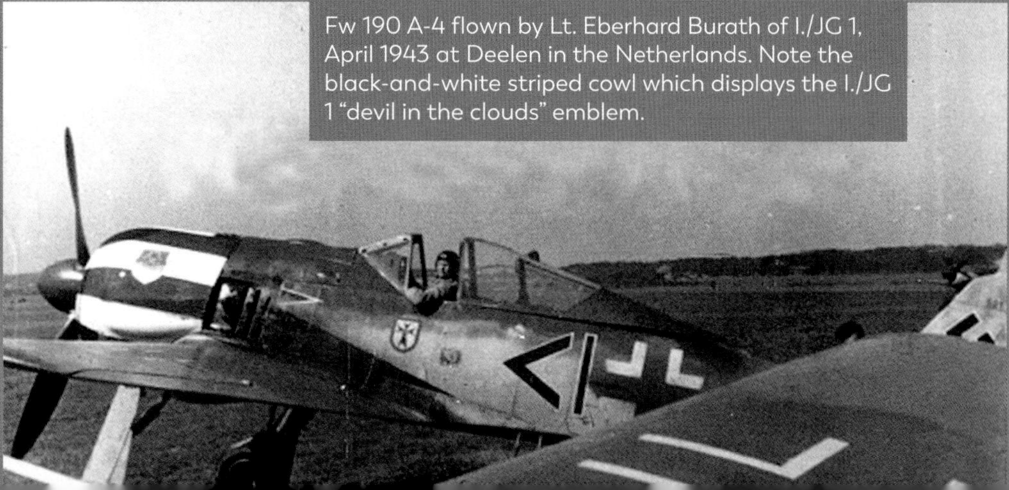

Fw 190 A-4 flown by Lt. Eberhard Burath of I./JG 1, April 1943 at Deelen in the Netherlands. Note the black-and-white striped cowl which displays the I./JG 1 "devil in the clouds" emblem.

In Profile:
Oesau, May, and Kirchmayr

Bf 109 G-6/AS, Kommodore JG 1 Oesau. Oberst Walter Oesau, one of the leading Luftwaffe fighter aces and commanders, was shot down and killed on May 11, 1944 near St. Vith at the controls of Bf 109 G-6/AS (W.Nr. 20601) Green 13. The G-6/AS ("S" for *Sonder* or "special") was powered by the DB 605 AS engine, a stop-gap development which featured a larger blower taken from the DB 603. The bigger intake required a larger port-side engine bearer arm which in turn resulted in the new refined cowl shape, the so-called asymmetrical *Ballungen* agglomeration ahead of the cockpit. The G-6 MG cowl "bulges" were dispensed with. It would appear that the sub-type was developed—aside from ongoing issues with the DB 605 D engine—to fulfil a high-altitude interceptor role, the so-called *Höhenjäger*, and were also notable for being finished in an overall 76 scheme *Höhenanstrich*.

Fw 190 A-3, 8./JG 2 Uffz. Friedrich May. May returned his first victory on June 10, 1942 and claimed two B-17s shot down at the end of the year. His sixth was a B-17 on December 30, 1942 during a raid by 1st Bombardment Wing B-17s attacking the U-boat pens at Lorient. On January 3, 1943 he shot down another B-17 and claimed two B-24s 20 km northwest of Brest, on April 16, 1943. Flying Fw 190 A-6 (W.Nr. 470047), he was killed on October 20, 1943 in the vicinity of Rouen in combat with Spitfires as an Oberfeldwebel with 3./JG 2. With at least 21 victories, May was awarded a posthumous German Cross in Gold.

Fw 190 A-7, Rüdiger von Kirchmayr, Staffelkapitän 5./JG 1, April–May 1944.

On July 25, 1943 the U.S. Eighth Air Force launched the series of operations known as *Blitz Week*. Ten targets in Germany were to be attacked during the next six days. Kiel and Hamburg were hit by over 200 B-17s on this day. Flying Fortresses of the 4th Bombardment Wing (BW) were attacked on their return by aircraft of I./JG 11 and Jasta Helgoloand. One Boeing was shot down at 16:55 by Lt. Hondt. Meanwhile, pilots of II./JG clashed with the B-17s of the 1st BW and managed to destroy three of them. Immediately after landing at Husum, the German fighters were refueled and rearmed. Forty minutes later most of them were airborne again. Over Helgoland they were joined by a Kette of Bf 109 Ts of Jasta Helgoland. Following a firing pass against the bombers, the pilots of II./JG 11 claimed four B-17s shot down. A fifth Fortress was claimed by Uffz. Turowski of Jasta Helgoland. The losses were four wounded pilots. The next day the Americans attacked Hamburg and Hanover. At around 11.00 a group of Boeings was attacked by Fw 190s of I./JG 11. The Germans managed to shoot down three Fortresses (Hptm. Clausen, Oblt. Grosser, and Fw. Doppler one each). Forty-five minutes later an American formation flying over Helgoland encountered aircraft of II./JG 11 and Bf 109 T-2s of Jasta Helgoland. The Germans managed to shoot down five B-17s; Hptm. Specht, Fw. Fürhrmann, Gefr. Lennhoff and Oblt. Adalbert Sommer (all from II./JG 11) destroyed one B-17 each. The fifth Fortress was added to the tally of Uffz. Doelling of Jasta Helgoland. Another Fortress was destroyed a few minutes later. Jasta Helgoland's Uffz. Erich Ulmschneider recalled:

> Suddenly we heard the droning of engines coming from the northeast and then, plowing through the sky at an altitude of 4,000 meters, we spotted the silhouette of an aircraft. It was a lone B-17 on its way back to England. The bomber had probably been damaged and forced from its formation. It was unlucky enough to find itself flying right past our base on Helgoland. Technicians leapt up onto the wing of my kite and cranked the inertia starter for all they were worth while I had never climbed into my cockpit so quickly—the last "Toni" left the airfield at full throttle. I was coaxing and cursing my kite in the same breath. "You lame duck, you beauty, you good 109, faster, faster!" As I closed to within 1,000 meters and prepared for an attack, I realized that the enemy had yet to make any defensive maneuvers, far less open up with defensive fire. Something was up with that bomber, perhaps there were wounded crew members aboard, since they would have surely noticed me by now. I got even closer to the Boeing; 400–500 meters more and I unleashed a burst of machine-gun fire. I stopped firing briefly and then let him have it from all barrels … Cease firing! What's happening now! I could see very clearly black spots tumbling away from the Boeing as the first parachutes popped open. The Boeing's captain must have realized the futility of this unequal fight and given the order to abandon the aircraft. I sighed with relief, as I was ready for a fierce fight. Having counted eight parachutes and observed the Boeing plunge into the sea, I dove away back to Helgoland with an unbelievable feeling of relief and joy in my heart: "You will not have them on your conscience!"

The bombers that had dropped their bombs over Hanover came under attack by JG 11 on their return. The following each claimed one B-17 destroyed: Fw. Zick, Maj. Mader, Hptm. Clausen, Oblt. Frey, and Oblt. Goetze. The Germans lost two pilots: Lt. Paul Arlt and Uffz. Walter Heisel.

On July 28, 1943, USAAF bombers attacked the Fieseler works at Kassel and AGO at Oschersleben. Once again, JG 11 was to intercept them on their ingress route. The Bf 109 Gs of II./JG 11 were the first to clash with the bombers. Eleven of them were armed with 250-kg bombs, Oblt. Knoke, Kapitän of 5. Staffel among them:

> After dropping the bombs, we got a fantastic view of what unfolded beneath us: the close-knit formation of bombers literally burst apart. Some Boeings plunged away in a steep dive, while others veered alarmingly out to the side, barely avoiding ramming each other. The bomb dropped by Fw. Fest fell bang in the middle of three bombers flying in a V formation. The three aircraft plummeted down almost simultaneously! Over 20 parachutes hung like mushrooms in the sky. There was some cheerful yelling in the headsets. It was amazing! Happy as never before, we flew loops and rolls over the enemy formation and it took us several minutes to calm down. "Jonny" Fest had downed three of them with one hit! Several other aircraft seemed to have been damaged. I encouraged my boys over the radio: "And now, we are going to kick their backsides! Go get them!" We fell upon the Amis from above in tight formation. I was flying a new machine armed with a 3-cm cannon. Its projectiles knocked huge holes in the Boeing's fuselage. The shocked pilot tried to evade my line of fire by violently nosing down. Five or six other enemy bombers, some of them in flames, veered out of the shattered formation, enabling us to pick them off one by one. One after the other tumbled down into the sea in flames. Huge burning slicks of gasoline appeared on the surface of the waves.

The pilots of II./JG 11 managed to shoot down 12 bombers in total. One Messerschmitt was hit by the Fortresses' defensive fire, but its pilot, Uffz. Erich Hoefig, managed to bail out. A few minutes after the II./JG Bf 109 Gs ended their attack, battle was joined by the Fw 190As of I./JG 11, whose pilots reported another six aircraft downed. Two were claimed by the Gruppenkommandeur, Hptm. Clausen. Again, there was only one German fighter lost and the pilot, Fw. Schmid, managed to bail out. From 10:00 to 11:00 several skirmishes between Rotten or Schwärme of JG 11 and the USAAF bombers took place with the German pilots reporting downing four Fortresses and one HSS. The last victory that day took place at 12.15 over Apeldoorn, where the Kapitän of 4. Staffel, Oblt. Sommer, shot down one Fortress on its way back to base.

A handful of III./ JG 3 Gustavs encountered their first B-17s on August 12, with Lt. Hans Schleef of 7./JG 3 claiming his 94th victory, a B-17 just north of Konigswinter. Five days later, on August 17, 1943, some 370 bombers set out on the first major USAAF daylight raid on Germany—the combined Schweinfurt–Regensburg mission, the so-called "Double Strike" raid on the ball-bearing and Messerschmitt production plants. The result was a disaster for the Americans: escorted only as far as the German border by P-47 Thunderbolts and RAF Spitfires, the Jagdgruppen launched wave after wave of attacks. Some 60 B-17s were shot down, only some 135 managing to return to friendly territory undamaged. (As Regensburg was only 40 miles from the Czech border, the 4th Bombardment Wing flew on to bases in North Africa.)

One "new" unit to hit the bombers was JG 50 under Maj. Hermann Graf. Initially established on July 21, 1943 as Jagdgruppe Süd der ObdL., a high-altitude fighter unit to combat the RAF's Mosquito twin-engined bomber and reconnaissance aircraft, by August its pilots were flying Werfer-Granate 21 rocket mortar-toting Bf 109s. Among Graf's pilots were three aces from his old Staffel, 9./JG 52: Oblt. Alfred Grislawski, Obfw. Ernst Süss, and

JG 50 was initially equipped with eight Bf 109 G-5s and Bf 109 G-6s, equipped with a special internal tank for liquefied nitrous oxide as part of the GM-1 engine power-boosting system, which was injected directly into the supercharger intake. This allowed the pilot to boost the rated horsepower of the DB 605 engine. Graf (on the tailplane) was allowed to pick any pilots he wished for the new unit.

Fw. Heinrich Füllgrabe. Oblt. Alfred Grislawski claimed two Fortresses on August 17, while on September 6 the unit shot down four over Stuttgart, one credited to Grislawski, and two claimed by Graf. Grislawski claimed one other kill, a B-17, on October 14. By October, JG 50 had been disbanded and merged with I. Gruppe JG 11. Graf was subsequently appointed Kommodore of JG 11 in November 1943. Two of the "Karaya Quartet" survived the war; Süss and Füllgrabe were killed in action.

In France, Oblt. "Sepp" Wurmheller, Staffelkapitän 9./ JG 2, was seriously injured on September 23, 1943 during a bombing raid on the airfield at Vannes. Airborne to counter

Kommandeur "Wutz" Galland II./JG 26 returning from a sortie. He was shot down by the B-17 fighter escort on the Schweinfurt–Regensburg raid, August 17, 1943.

a 1st Bombardment Division raid on Nantes, the Staffelkapitän of 9./ JG 2 landed back at Vannes just as the airfield came under attack from another wave of bombers. Wurmheller scrambled down from the cockpit of his machine just moments before it was obliterated by a direct hit. He was seriously wounded by shrapnel.

On October 4, 1943, Hptm. Erwin Clausen's luck ran out. After months of fighting in JG 77, he had been promoted to command I./JG 11 on June 20, 1943. On October 4, he went missing near Borkum after shooting down his 132nd victim, one of 11 B-17s on his scoreboard. Clausen had received the Knight's Cross and Oak Leaves in July 1942.

Fw 190 Yellow 11 of 6./JG 26, June 1943 at Vitry-en-Artois. Fw. Petersen (hands in pockets) chats with Ofw. Meyer in the cockpit

On October 7, at a conference at Berchtesgaden, Göring relayed the Führer's dissatisfaction with the performance of the fighter pilots over Germany to his Gruppenkommandeure and sent out new orders to the *Jagdflieger* defending the Reich: 1) There are no weather conditions in which the fighter pilots cannot get airborne; 2) Any fighter pilot returning without a victory or in an undamaged machine shall appear before a court martial; and 3) Any *Jagdflieger* who runs out of muntions or is unable to use his onboard armament must ram the enemy bombers. The following day the Kommodore JG 1, Obstlt. Hans Philipp, responded to his formation

Preparing an Fw 190 A-5 of the Stab JG 26 for a sortie—ground crew "black men" are seen removing the tarps covering the cowl and plugging in the electric starter cart.

leaders at Deelen: "I refuse to answer to or to be judged by a court martial—I know what I have to do."

Leading JG 1 that same afternoon against an Eighth Air Force raid against Bremen, Philipp was shot down and disappeared near Nordhorn. He had just returned his 206th victory—the sole B-17 on his scoreboard—after a frontal attack on a *Pulk* when his Fw 190 was seen to be hit and catch fire before disappearing into the clouds. His last words heard over the frequency were an exhortation to his wingman, Fw. Hans-G Reinhardt—himself a 44-victory ace—to attack the bombers. His position was taken over for a time by Maj. Graf and then by Obstlt. Walter Oesau. Philipp's loss was probably the hardest blow to the Tagjagd fighting in the Reichsverteidigung, the defense of the Reich. Four days later, the 26-year-old ace was buried with full military honors in his hometown—the Führer himself sent a wreath and a hand-signed message of condolence.

I./JG 11 under Oblt. Erich Hondt in his Focke Wulf A-5/U12 Black 13 mounting two extra underwing gondolas each fitted with two 2-cm cannon, sighted the bomber formations over the Dutch coast:

> with a shout of "*Hinein!*"—"In we go!"—my Staffel dove head-on into the *Pulks* with a height advantage of some 1,500 meters. I counted five of them, each comprising 50 machines. I opened up on a Boeing in the first *Pulk*, dove through the second and got another Boeing in my sights in the third *Pulk* and let him have it. Suddenly there was a bang and my hands were torn off the control column, fingers hanging down loosely from a strip of flesh, blood everywhere. At the same time, I took a huge blow to the chin. I couldn't operate the firing button and all the time the B-17 was looming larger in my sight. In my rage I tipped over onto the right wing and my left wing scythed into the bomber's wing between the two engines on the port side. There was a terrific crash, my head slammed

Funeral cortège of Kommodore JG 1 Obstlt. Hans Philipp in his hometown of Meissen, October 14, 1943. The coffin is escorted by Philipp's Geschwader comrades.

> into the gunsight and my machine started to tumble earthward, engine screaming, flames licking from under the cowl. *Aussteigen!* Get out! I tried to free my belt but couldn't use my hands. I noticed the flames had burned through my flying suit. I could feel the terrible heat through my flight goggles and oxygen mask. At that point I gave up.

Hondt somehow survived the attack and the crash; as it turned out, moments later his machine exploded, throwing him clear. Miraculously, his 'chute deployed and he landed safely. He had sustained 60-percent burns but was back on operations over Normandy in June 1944.

On October 14, return fire from a B 17 fatally injured leading III./JG 3 ace Alfred Surau. During the summer of 1943 Surau was briefly one of the most effective aces in 9. Staffel. He scored his first victory on February 28, 1943, while flying on the Russian front. When III./JG 3 was transferred to the Western Front by a Luftwaffe leadership nervous at the ever-growing strength of the U.S. Eighth Air Force buildup in the UK, Surau's claims had reached 41 in just six months. His run of success was not to last though. As was Luftwaffe practice, this last "victory" was "officially" confirmed. He had been awarded a German Cross in Gold in September.

On November 3, after a fierce battle with P-47s defending B-17s, Maj. Kurt Brändle, a 1937 veteran leading II./JG 3, was shot down at sea west of Amsterdam. He had 180 victories to his credit (25 in the West) and had received the Oak Leaves on August 27, 1942.

There was another heavy loss on November 25, 1943 when Maj. Johannes Seifert, leading II./JG 26, was killed near Estaires, colliding with the P-38 Lightning he had just shot

Staffelkapitän 2./JG 11 Erich Hondt's Fw 190 A-5 (W.Nr. 410266) Black 13 wore the so-called *Schwarmführerstreifen*, the Schwarm leader's red diagonal stripes along the fuselage appearing as a V from above; it may also have had a yellow *Rumpf* or fuselage band. Hondt's A-5 was also fitted with the U12 *Rüstsatz* (field modification kit) which consisted of underwing gondolas, each containing a pair of MG 151 cannon, one of the few armament *Rüstsätze* to reach operational status.

Bf 109 G-6/R6 (W.Nr. 18807) Yellow 6, Ofw. Alfred Surau, 9./JG 3, Bad Wörishofen, September 1943. This aircraft is fitted with the underwing *Rüstsatz VI* gondola cannon kit which consisted of two 2-cm Mauser MG 151/20 underwing gunpods with 135 rpg. Note also the tall antenna mast; the loop for the DF set, or *Peilrufgerät*, only started to appear from the summer of 1943.

down (57th victory). Seifert had fought in Poland in a ZG (destroyer wing) but very quickly joined the "Schlageter." In June 1942, he received the Knight's Cross and was then withdrawn from the front following a *Führeranlass*, a special decree, his brother having been killed in III./JG 26. He had returned to the front at his own request.

These bloody battles against the USAAF overshadowed the battles that continued to take place in countering RAF incursions, however here too losses were serious: On March 13, near Tréport, Hptm. Heinrich Setz, now Kommandeur I./JG 27, died at the controls of his Bf 109 G-4. Another 1939 veteran and Oak Leaves bearer with II./JG 77 in the East, Setz had 138 victories to his credit and reportedly downed three Spitfires before his death.

On May 15, Lt. Horst Hannig shot down a Spitfire (his 98th *Luftsieg*) near Rocquancourt but also had to abandon his Fw 190. His parachute failed to deploy. Having operated mainly in the East with 6./JG 54, he received the Knight's Cross in May 1942 for 48 victories but had only eight in the West since his transfer in January 1943 to 2./JG 2 as Kapitän. He received the Oak Leaves posthumously.

Despite the difficulties in bringing the necessary firepower to bear against the Flying Fortresses, the Tagjagd could often strike them hard. Here, a 95th BG Fortress has been brought down on August 12, 1943 at Mützenich during an attack on the Ruhr.

Hptm. Walter Dahl led III./JG 3 later in 1943. He is seen dismounting from his usual Gustav at Bad Wörishofen. He survived the war with around 100 victories, including an unknown number of four-engined bombers. This pilot's tally is often exaggerated, originating from his post-war memoir *Rammjäger*. Dahl was awarded the Oak Leaves in February 1945 for 92 victories.

On September 4, Oblt. Kurt Goltzsch, leading 5./JG 2, was shot down near Monchy-le-Preux. Sustaining spinal injuries, he was extracted from the wreck of his 109 G-6 and spent long months in hospital before dying on September 26, 1944. Credited with 43 victories, he was awarded the Knight's Cross in February 1944 in his hospital bed. On September 11, another veteran, Lt. Hugo Dahmer, was seriously wounded in combat near Rouen. A month earlier, this former JG 5 "Eismeer" ace had taken over 1./JG 2. Now prohibited from flying, this 45-victory ace (including one *Viermot*) went on to a training school and survived the war.

Kommandeur Dahl salutes pilots of the *Werferstaffel* in front of White 6, Bf 109 G-6 (W.Nr. 26025), which is having its engine run-up.

The Mediterranean, 1943

Surrounded in its Tunisian redoubt, the Panzerarmee Afrika was to fight its last battles. The Luftwaffe did everything it could to supply the pocket and repatriate the wounded, while the Tagjagd tried to repel the Anglo-American bombers.

In November 1942, Oblt. Adolf Dickfeld was appointed Gruppenkommandeur of II./JG 2 on the Western Front. Born on February 20, 1920 in Breslau (Wroclaw), Dickfeld entered the war as a Leutnant in I./JG 52 and, after being transferred to III./JG 52 and participating in the invasion of Russia, his tally began to grow rapidly. During fierce fighting in the southern sector of the Eastern Front in the spring of 1942 he had some spectacular successes. On May 14 he managed to shoot down nine enemy machines, raising his tally to 90, and four days later he managed to destroy another 11, becoming the eighth Luftwaffe pilot to score 100 aerial victories. He was awarded the Oak Leaves on May 19, 1942 for 101 victories and promoted Oberleutnant on May 21, 1942. He arrived at JG 2 to be met by Kommodore Oesau. As Dickfeld himself recalled: "Kommodore Oesau welcomed me at Beaumont-le-Roger with 'What do you want first, the good news or the bad news?'" I didn't mind. 'Well, the good news is, you're only staying three days here. The bad news is, you're going to Africa!' I nearly fell off my chair."

Dickfeld achieved five victories over Tunisia, including a Blenheim on November 30, 1942, a Spitfire on December 1, and a P-38 on December 3, before he was badly injured in a takeoff accident at Kairouan on January 8, 1943, when his Fw 190 A-4 (W.Nr. 0750) ran into a bomb crater and overturned as he was attempting to get airborne during a raid on the airfield. On April 17, 1943, after recovering from his injuries, Dickfeld was appointed Gruppenkommandeur II./JG 11, based in the Bremen–Helgoland area of northern Germany performing RVT duties.

Jules Meimberg arrived in North Africa in late 1942 with 11./JG 2. Subordinated to the Stab II./JG 53, his Staffel flew out of Bizerte in the far north of Tunisia before redeploying to Tunis-El Aouina. He returned his 31st victory somewhat fortuitously as he himself recounted:

Oblt. Adolf Dickfeld.

Despite setbacks, the atmosphere could still be cheerful at I./JG 77. From left: Lt. Karl Eberle (2./JG 77, eight victories, face just visible), Lt. Arminius Köhler (future Knight's Cross bearer), Hptm. Bär (Kommandeur I./JG 77), Oblt. Heinz-Edgar Berres (future Knight's Cross winner). Oblt. Ernst Laube (Kapitän 3./JG 77, eight victories) is just out of shot here.

Fw 190 A-4 of II./JG 2 being inspected by locals, at Tindja near Cap Blanc on the northern coast of Tunisia. Oblt. Adolf Dickfeld is standing under the dark-painted spinner—note the stylized "eagle-wing" exhaust marking.

A veteran of 1940, Obfw. Herbert Kaiser (center) had flown with III./JG 77. By the end of January 1943, he had been evacuated from Tunsia completely exhausted and sent as an instructor to the Er. JGr. Süd in Marseilles. On March 14, 1943, at Marignane airfield, he was awarded the Knight's Cross for his 54 victories by the school's commander, Obstlt. Alfred Müller (right), a former Great War pilot. Kaiser returned to JG 77 and then JG 1, finishing the war with 68 victories. At left is Oblt. Erwin Clausen, a JG 77 comrade also attached to the school as an instructor.

Staka 11./JG 2. Jules Meimberg alights from his Bf 109 G-2 on his return from a sortie, at Bizerte. His Staffel was subordinated to JG 53.

> it was the last day of January 1943 and I was up over Tunis on my own on a flight test when our lead officer radioed that a high-flying recce machine was reported heading over the city. I soon caught sight of it—a small glint in the sky that I was able to close on undetected. It was a Lightning. This was my first encounter with this twin-engined twin-boom fighter. Seeger had already warned me that they were not to be underestimated. And he was right: when I opened up on him at an altitude of 7,500 meters, the American caught me by surprise, hauling into such a tight turn to come around and face me that I could barely believe it. He had thrown down the gauntlet and I was amazed at his roll rate and maneuverability. But I managed to unleash the decisive strikes, timed at 13:00 and, although wounded, my opponent bailed out and was taken captive.

However, the next day, February 1, 1943, luck abandoned "Jules" Meimberg: scrambled with 11./JG 2 at around midday, Meimberg's high-altitude interceptors were directed onto a formation of a dozen unescorted B-17s approaching Tunis. This was another opportunity for Meimberg to trial his *Frontalangriff* head-on attack tactic. The B-17 gunners' concentrated defensive fire quickly turned the cockpit of his Bf 109 into a *Flammenmeer*—a sea of flames—and by the time he had managed to extricate himself from his stricken machine, he had sustained serious burns. A downed B-17 was credited to Meimberg although no four-engined bomber was lost over Tunis that day. Just days later Meimberg was repatriated to Germany to convalesce. When he returned to 6./ JG 53 in August 1943, 11./JG 2 was no more and the Germans had been expelled from North Africa.

On February 23, 1943, Kairouan was raided by B-17s of the 301st BG. Gruppenführer II./JG 2 Erich Rudorffer recalled:

Lt. Rolf Schlegel of 4./JG 53 in his G-6 "Trop" White 6. He returned nine victories.

One of the last photos taken of Maj. Joachim Müncheberg, seen here looking over his new Gustav.

we were scrambled at 08:38 on the approach of a formation of U.S. bombers. It was my task to keep Wolf von Bülow, Staffelkapitän of 5./ JG 2, out of the action as much as I could. This was because Wolf was the son of our former Kommodore, who had already lost his other son, a U-boat commander. So he only flew so many sorties and on this occasion he did not scramble with us. In the end it proved more dangerous on the ground than in the air—a stick of bombs came down on his foxhole, right where he had sought shelter. Oblt. von Bülow's body was riddled with shrapnel. His death was a terrible blow to morale. In any case the atmosphere within the unit was going downhill fast following Dickfeld's departure. There was far too much bad feeling and competitiveness around aerial victories and the scramble for decorations and promotion had become far too important and such a state of affairs could only harm any esprit de corps.

The most significant loss in North Africa occurred on March 23, 1943, when the Kommodore of JG 77, Maj. Joachim Müncheberg, made his 500th *Feindflug* (operational sortie). He shot down a Spitfire (135th victory) near Maknassy but his Bf 109 G-6 was itself hit by debris and brought down. Müncheberg thus perished in the African theater where he had cemented his reputation two years earlier when he led 7./JG 26. In his honor, the Geschwader adopted the badge of this Staffel: a red heart. His successor came from the East: Maj. Johannes Steinhoff, former Kommandeur of II./ JG 52. During his first sortie in African skies, the new Kommodore was shot down but was able to put his 109 down on its belly.

Maj. Johannes Steinhoff (left) arrived in North Africa from the East as the new Kommodore of JG 77, replacing Müncheberg.

At JG 53, Lt. Wilhelm Crinius and Hptm. Wolfgang Tonne, who had just distinguished themselves in the USSR, could no longer do the same in the face of the Allied air superiority. On January 13, 1943, Crinius (114 victories) was to land near La Calle after falling prey to a Spitfire and ended the war in captivity. On April 20, Tonne won his 121st and 122nd near Tunis but was killed in a crash shortly afterward at Bizerte. On January 14, near Buerat, Obfw. Walter Brandt of 2./JG 77 (a 1939 veteran) won his 37th victory before being shot down in turn. Having had a leg amputated, he was subsequently transferred to the Reich and awarded the Knight's Cross in March at the hospital. Despite his serious handicap, he continued to fly with an artificial limb, leading 2./JG 3 and adding five *Luftsiege* to his tally.

Tunisia was evacuated in early May. Africa was lost for the Axis. One of the last aircraft to take off from the continent for Sicily was a Bf 108 from JG 77, on May 8. The overloaded aircraft left the ground at Korbous before crashing and killing its crew. The pilot was Oblt. Helmut Meckel, a I./JG 3 *Experte* with 25 victories. He had received the Knight's Cross in August 1941 but was soon forced to leave the front due to his injuries. In early 1943, he asked to join the Stab/JG 77 where he was to serve as a pilot on liaison aircraft. His comrades buried him alongside the runway with his unfortunate companions.

It was on Sicily that the Wehrmacht awaited the next invasion. Aerial reconnaissance took place regularly and, during one of these missions, Hptm. Günther Hannak, leading 7./JG 27, had to land in Malta after engine trouble. This ace, with 47 victories, and holder of the Knight's Cross, was taken captive.

In the run-up to the invasion of Sicily, the island was pounded by large fleets of bombers from Africa. Some in Berlin viewed the performance of a numerically inferior Tagjagd force as being decidely below par. An example was the clash that took place on June 25. A formation of 100 B-17s without fighter escort was detected by German radar and some 80 Bf 109 Gs were scrambled for a radar-guided intercept. In the ensuing battle just one B-17 was shot down, credited to Kommodore Steinhoff, while the Germans lost one of their Bf 109s. When Göring was told about this débâcle, he furiously ordered that one pilot from each Gruppe should be court-martialed for cowardice. As Kommodore JG 77 Steinhoff recalled:

> We were gathered in the mess … Galland had called to tell me that the Reichsmarschall was unhappy and thought we had failed. I had to tell the men

Inspector of Fighters Adolf Galland came to Sicily following the German setbacks. He is seen here accompanied by a grim-faced Oberst Günther Lützow.

Oblt. Siegfried Freytag, the "Lion of Malta" and Kapitän of 1./JG 77. Courageous and often contemptuous of authority, Freytag was admired by the vast majority of his subordinates. He was awarded the Knight's Cross in July 1942 for 57 victories. Freytag survived the war and went on to serve with the French Foreign Legion.

Kommandeur Bär I./JG 77 (right) with Lt. Armin Köhler, a future Knight's Cross bearer.

Early 1943, Sicily. Bär with the lion cub mascot lent by Leipzig Zoo—it was later returned when it got too big.

> that one pilot from each Gruppe had to be brought before a court martial for—and suddenly the words stuck in my throat—"cowardice in the face of the enemy." A deathly silence fell over the entire table. They looked at me incredulously. It was Freytag who found his voice first. He raised his glass and said: "Good! Good! *Prost! Prost!* I volunteer!" I could have taken him in my arms. With his biting irony, he had shown the way to us commanders.

While the charges trumped up against those pilots threatened with court martial eventually came to nothing, stupidity of this kind was obvious. It marked the end of the relationship between the high command and the operational base, betrayed as it was by blinkered superiors in Berlin and which largely explains the drop in morale among the Tagjäger in southern Italy. This order also largely tarnished the reputation of Adolf Galland, an excellent combat pilot, but apparently a detestable senior officer. In his account of the fighting over Sicily Steinhoff painted a striking portrait of Freytag:

On June 1, 1943, with Tunisia evacuated and the Allies preparing to land on Sicily, Lt. Gerd Hanf was posted to 9. Staffel of JG 77 on Sardinia:

> I was assigned a Bf 109 G-6 with two additional cannon slung under the wings and a large drop tank under the fuselage. So this *lahmarschige Krahe*—lame-assed crow—was the latest model of Bf 109? With a great deal of effort, it could do 350 kph but never got near 400 kph. The cockpit was so narrow and confined that I could barely move. Sorties were flown with the obligatory life jacket and signal cartridges, but would that be enough? I was subsequently assigned Yellow 2 which had been shot up several times but always came home "even when the pilot was wounded" or so I was told. During June 1943 the thermometer often showed 40°C in the shade and the aircraft got so hot that you couldn't touch them. The heat was unbearable. It determined how our daily routine was organized; maintenance was done at night once the aircraft had cooled off a little and the *Feldküche* only served food after 22:00. Nobody had any appetite during the day. On June 18 I was caught up in my first air combat—III./ JG 77 intercepted a formation of B-25s escorted by P-38 fighters. As a greenhorn I quickly lost sight of what was happening, and, worse, lost my Rottenführer. There was soon an almighty bang in the cockpit as a round hit the fuselage and partially shredded the instrument panel, sending splinters everywhere. I had a few scratches and cuts but managed to get back to the field. Safely on the ground I was told, "There, you see, Yellow 2 always comes home!"

Yellow 16 of 9./ JG 77, at Chilivani, Sardinia, during the summer of 1943. The small yellow *Kennziffer* and the *Wander Zirkus Ubben* (lit. the Ubben wandering circus) Gruppe emblem of III./JG 77 have been added to an overpainted area on the fuselage. This G-6 has a white prop spiral and a sand filter over the intake.

Bf 109 G-6 "Trop" of JG 53 force-landed on a Sicilian beach but could not be recovered prior to the American landings; it is seen here being inspected by U.S. troops. Note the underwing cannon pods and the white theater fuselage band.

> Freytag appeared tired and even at the end of his nerves; a mop of his very blond hair fell across his face, hiding his sweaty forehead … He was 23 years old, he was a born pilot but he was as skittish as a thoroughbred racehorse. Everyone in the unit knew he was drinking and even drunk every night. He lived in fear of being caught in a bombing raid … But he never gave up on a mission.

On July 10, 1943, Operation *Husky*, the landings in Sicily, began and the German garrison evacuated. German fighters struggled to furnish cover for the German withdrawal, let alone achieve any success.

On July 17, near Catania, British antiaircraft fire shot down the Bf 109 G-6 flown by Oberleutnant and Knight's Cross bearer Wolf Ettel, leading 8./JG 27. Ettel had started his career in the summer of 1942 and was credited with 120 victories in the East plus four in

La Marsa, April 1943. Kapitän of 4./JG 53 Fritz Dinger (center), and Kommandeur II./ JG 53, Hptm. Gerhard Michalski (right) in discussion with their men. Dinger was killed during an Allied bombing raid on Sicily. Shortly before his death, he had been given time off to get married. His 53rd victory was returned in December 1942 and his 54th on March 22, 1943.

Alarmstart! Pilots scramble, probably in Tunisia. Dinger's White 4 and Ofw. Stefan Litjens' White 5 can be seen.

the West. He was killed while strafing an enemy position. On July 25, over Milazzo, Oblt. Heinz-Edgar Berres, leading 1./JG 77, was shot down by a Spitfire during a Ju 52 escort mission. Berres, who arrived at the unit in 1941, had 52 *Abschüsse* and received the Knight's Cross posthumously. On July 27, the small airfield at Scalea was bombed. Oblt. Fritz Dinger, Kapitän of 4./JG 53, was killed by shrapnel. He had 67 victories to his credit, 25 of which were in the Mediterranean, and wore the Knight's Cross. It should be noted that two JG 77 aces, Oblt. Emil Omert and Obfw. Ernst-Wilhelm Reinert, were also victims of antiaircraft fire over Sicily but both resumed their careers.

Thanks to excellent organization, the Wehrmacht evacuated the island without too many casualties. But continental airfields then became targets for Allied bombers while the Germans kept half an eye on an unreliable Italian ally. On September 2, the Austrian Hptm. Franz Schiess led his 8./JG 53 against P-38s at sea off Ischia but was reported missing. A Knight's Cross bearer since 21 June 1943, he had 67 victories to his credit (21 in Africa and three *Viermots*).

On September 8, Italy changed sides, forcing Hitler to close down the *Citadel* operation in the East. The Allies were able to come ashore at Salerno without too much difficulty and move northward. German troops, well led by the Oberbefehlshaber Süd, Marshal Albert Kesselring, locked down the roads leading north and the Tagjagd was engaged over the successive front lines. Although numerically inferior, the Luftwaffe would have some respite and be able to take onto its inventory the booty taken from the Italian Air Force.

At the end of 1943, III./JG 77 left for Romania to take over from I./JG 4, which had been less tested, while the latter reinforced the Tagjagd in Italy. The recently established IV./JG 3, also engaged in Italy, suffered losses such as that of Oblt. Gustav Frielinghaus, leading 11./JG 3, shot down by P-38s near Foggia. Seriously wounded, he received the Knight's Cross in hospital for his 74 *Luftsiege* (won mainly in the East). Victim of a subsequent accident, he did not fly again but commanded various ground units.

In September 1943, Britain, trying to take advantage of the Italian surrender, attempted to gain a foothold in the Dodecanese islands. Unfortunately for them, the capture of the

Bf 109 G-6s of III./JG 27 flying escort over the Aegean Sea. They would be very active over the Dodecanese in late 1943. White 2 is flown by Uffz. Emil Clade.

Two Bf 109 F-4 "Trop" Friedrichs Red 3 and Red 5 of 8./ JG 27 at readiness on Maritsa airfield, Rhodes. Note the striped camouflage effect over the wings.

8./ JG 27 deployed from Crete to Rhodes in mid-Janury 1943 for some six weeks, tasked with intercepting British torpedo bombers attacking German and Italian shipping running supplies to islands throughout the Aegean. Fw. Arthur Liebhold poses on his Red 3.

island of Rhodes, with its good aerodromes, failed. The Luftwaffe dominated the sky and the Royal Navy the sea. After several weeks of fighting, German bombers and paratroopers—well supported by III. and IV. /JG 27—forced the British to surrender.

JG 53 underwent a major change when its Kommodore, Freiherr von Maltzahn, exhausted and sick with malaria, and the CO of the "Pik As" since the Battle of Britain, left the unit on October 4. He was replaced by Obstlt. Helmut Bennemann. With 88 victories, this former Kommandeur of I./JG 52 had returned from convalescence after being burned by an incendiary bomb. In October, II./JG 53 was deployed to Vienna to protect Austria from Allied incursions from the south.

Allied aircraft attacking northern Italy from all sides were regularly intercepted in the Balkans. On December 17, 1943, during one of these encounters, the Bf 109 G-6 flown

On February 11, 1943 Oblt. Werner Schroer, Kommandeur III./JG 27, donned his best uniform to fly back to Crete to get married; during the course of the flight he claimed two British Beauforts.

Obfw. Rudolf Ehrenberger, II./JG 53 ace, had flown with the Gruppe since 1940. On March 20, 1943, he shot down two enemy aircraft to record his 33rd and 34th victories. He recorded his 40th victory on June 9. By September, his score stood at forty-three.

by the Kommandeur of IV./JG 27, the Saxon Hptm. Joachim Kirschner, was shot down in Bosnia. Captured by Tito's partisans, this 188-victory Knight's Cross bearer was executed at Stolac. Kirschner, who joined the Luftwaffe in October 1939, had flown mainly with II./JG 3 and had only assumed his last command two months earlier. He was holder of the Oak Leaves and had won 20 victories in the West (including two four-engined bombers).

Hptm. Joachim Kirschner (left) was executed by Yugoslav partisans. Here he is seen being congratulated on his 150th victory by II./JG 3 Kommandeur Kurt Brändle.

In Profile:
Hartmann, Kutscha, and Müller

Bf 109 G-10, Erich Hartmann, tulip marking, April 1945. Possibly Hartmann's last machine, a G-10 which featured a black tulip painted on the nose. Everything aft of the fuselage cross is still guesswork although contemporary I./JG 52 aircraft show no yellow bands or rudders. The smaller-size fuselage cross was introduced by Erla somewhere during the production run of their G-10 series. The lower surfaces may have been left in natural metal.

Bf 109 G-6 Yellow 13, Staffelkapitän 12./JG 3 Oblt. Herbert Kutscha, February 1944. Kutscha earned his Knight's Cross with II./ZG 1 in the East. IV./JG 3 operated in concert with the Sturmstaffel from Salzwedel during February–April 1944. Kutscha was shot down by P-47s near Venlo on February 23, 1944 and was out of action for several months.

Bf 109 G-6 "Doppelwinkel" with Erla Haube flown by Kommandeur IV./JG 3 Maj. Friedrich-Karl Müller, early 1944, Salzwedel. Müller had served as Kommandeur I./JG 53 in Italy and the East and on his arrival at IV./JG 3 had been credited with 118 victories and awarded the Oak Leaves. He claimed three *Viermots* on March 8 for his victories 119–121. Appointed Kommodore JG 3, he was killed at Salzwedel on May 29, 1944 when his Bf 109 stalled and crashed during a landing approach.

Lt. Alfred Hammer's G-6 "Trop" Yellow 1 fitted with cannon pods seen on the Italian mainland at Cancello, August 1943. He was appointed Staffelkapitän of 6./JG 53 on July 28, 1943. At the end of the war he led IV./JG 53, flying his last sortie on April 20, 1945, for a total of 463 sorties and 26 confirmed kills.

In the south of the Italian boot, German fighter units were relentlessly hunted down by Allied bombers, like here at Cancello where many II./JG 53 Bf 109s went up in smoke in raids that took place on September 4 and 5.

At Kalamaki airfield Fw. Heinrich Bartels poses alongside his rudder scoreboard on his G-6 Red 13. The leading *Experte* of 11./JG 27 returned his 70th victory on November 15, 1943. He arrived in Greece during August 1943 from JG 5 where he had been awarded the Knight's Cross on November 13, 1942.

The West and the Reich, 1944

Following the disastrous losses sustained on the September 6, 1943 in the Schweinfurt–Regensburg raid—the largest USAAF daylight raid to date—there was something of a lull in the USAAF bombing campaign. Only later on in the year and through early 1944 did the USAAF feel strong enough to attempt similar heavy raids. One crucial factor made the difference: by late 1943 Allied fighters now had enough range to escort bombers into the Reich. 1944 would mark the high point of the so-called Allied Combined Bomber Offensive against the German Reich, with well over a million tons of bombs dropped.

Luftflotte Reich had a fighter force of some 550 machines of which just over 400 were serviceable on January 1, 1944, among some 19 Tagjagdgruppen, each of which could barely muster more than 20 machines. The primary task of these fighters was to destroy as many *Viermots* as possible while defending themselves from the swarms of agile escort fighters.

On January 11, a huge formation of 633 bombers headed for the Junkers, Focke-Wulf, and Messerschmitt plants at Oschersleben, Halberstadt, and Braunschweig in central Germany. The bombers were assigned an escort comprised of 592 fighters, but due to heavy overcast cloud, the rendezvous was missed and the bombers were recalled. Around half of them pressed on, eventually breaking through banks of thick cloud into clear blue skies. The "welcoming committee" of over 239 Luftwaffe fighters was presented with excellent conditions to launch attack after attack. The Germans even threw their night fighters into the battle. Over 100 U.S. bombers were claimed destroyed. Among those which fell prey

Kommandeur III./JG 3 Walther Dahl in the cockpit of a 9. Staffel Gustav Yellow 1, Leipheim, January 1944. Dahl was awarded the Knight's Cross in March 1944.

to pilots of II./JG 27 were four Pathfinder Liberators, which had been performing the role for the first time. The Gruppe's commander, Hptm. Schroer, brought down two of them. JG 11 attacked the bomber formations as early as the Dutch–German border. I./JG 11 returned one victory and an HSS while losing one machine (its pilot unharmed) in an initial attack. II./JG 11 pilots reported 11 victories. Their own losses were also serious: eight Messerschmitts downed. Three pilots died, three were wounded. Lt. Georg Wroblewski of 5./JG 11 recalled:

> We attacked a large box of B-17s. They had no fighter cover, so we closed for the attack from directly astern with the advantage of height. I was flying too fast to open fire on the B-17s flying at the rear of the formation, therefore—rather stupidly—I skirted close by the whole group to attack the Boeing flying at the head of the formation's right wing. I got some good hits on it because I flew through a hail of fragments, whirling off the aircraft's structure in the slipstream. One of the pieces of debris slammed into my left wing. I had to bail out a few seconds later—my 109 was burning and my leg was starting to hurt badly. I suspect I took a round in my leg probably while I was passing the formation as I had felt a light strike but no pain. I heard nothing more about the Boeing I hit, so I never reported it as a kill. Besides, I felt very rough for about a week or so.

The fighters of III./JG 11 that attacked the bombers at 11:30 west of Hildesheim did not encounter any fighter cover either. It was thus possible for them to mount several attacks, shooting down eight four-engined bombers and returning an HSS. The German losses were five aircraft and three pilots killed.

Seven heavy bombers were claimed by III./JG 54 under Hptm. Siegfried Schnell, which at that time was subordinated to JG 26. Fw. Friedrich Ungar of 9./JG 54, flying his Bf 109 G-6/U4 Yellow 6, scored his first victory in somewhat extraordinary circumstances. He recalled:

> The silhouettes of the B-17s ahead of us quickly grew larger. Their gunners opened up—I noticed little white puffs coming out of the barrels. Finally, we were within range. I opened fire at a distance of 800 meters, closing to 600 meters, whereupon I broke off the attack and pulled up sharp. I could not observe any effects of my fire. This was my very first attack on bombers. I altered course and left the

Fw 190 A-7 flown by Lt. Hans Schrangl of I./JG 11 being refueled and rearmed at Rothenburg. Strangl claimed some ten *Viermots* shot down in early 1944.

Hptm. Günther Specht's Bf 109 G-5/AS, "decorated" for his award of the Knight's Cross on April 8, 1944; note the decoration over the cowl. Specht was Gruppenkommandeur II./JG 11; his 29th and 30th victories were achieved over Detmold on February 22, 1944 (a P-51 and a B-17). With some 15 heavy bombers destroyed, he was one of the leading "bomber killers" in the defense of the Reich, despite having lost his left eye.

> bomber formation behind. I was surprised that my aircraft hadn't sustained any serious damage, for I was in the middle of an enemy formation studded with twin-mounted guns and the gunners manning them were doing their best to riddle me with bullets.
>
> And what's this? Before I could join the rest of my Staffel, I spotted a lone B-17 heading south. It must have dropped out of formation during the momentary confusion caused by our pass and ended up to the right of its combat box. It wasn't aflame, neither was it trailing smoke. I couldn't see any battle damage either. Apparently, fate was giving me, a greenhorn, the chance to practice a textbook attack on a Flying Fortress. Moreover, there was not a single escort fighter to be seen in the vicinity.
>
> I immediately settled myself some 300 meters above the bomber and rammed forward the throttle lever, attacking with height advantage. At a distance of 600 meters I levelled with the enemy. I was flying much faster than the bomber and from 400 meters I set his right outboard engine on fire. Moments later I saw two men bail out. The starboard wing erupted in flames, which indicated that I had hit the fuel tank. Since I saw no defensive fire, I slowly passed by the Fortress. When I found myself some 1,000 meters ahead of the bomber, I decided to make another pass, this time headlong. Again, I brought my guns to bear on the right outboard engine. I saw four more crewmembers take to their parachutes. The bomber was abandoned. I wasn't sure, but it seemed they hadn't jettisoned their bombload.
>
> For a few moments the B-17 kept a steady course, then slowly dropped its nose and began to descend until it fell into a steep dive. At 11:30 it slammed into the ground on the edge of a forest, west of Ockensen, some 40 km south of Hanover. A pall of dirt and smoke kicked high up in the sky, marking the spot where I had scored my first aerial victory.

After a spell of bad weather, January 29 saw another massive raid: 863 bombers with 632 escorts flew against industrial and rail targets in Frankfurt am Main. American losses amounted to 26 machines, including 12 bombers, but as many as 40 German fighters failed to return. One of them was Bf 109 G-6 (W.Nr. 440073) Yellow 3 flown by Oblt. Wilhelm "Willy" Kientsch,

In Profile:
Sturmstaffel 1

As USAAF bomber raids intensified over the Continent, a radical new air-fighting concept was conceived by a 37-year-old former fighter pilot, Maj. Günther von Kornatzki. Gruppenkommandeur of II./JG 52 during the Battle of Britain, he surmised that a special type of fighter unit be established to bring down bombers by ramming if all else failed, inflicting the sorts of losses that might put a stop to the Allied bombing campaign. General of Fighters Adolf Galland decided that this close-in fighting or *Sturm* ("storm" or "assault") idea should be tested and a modified concept was quickly outlined. Evading the escort fighters, heavily armed and armored *Sturm* Focke-Wulf 190 fighters were to fly mass attacks in large, wedge-shaped, line-abreast formations—*Angriffskeil*—closing from astern, and only opening up at close range with their heavy cannon to make certain of a kill. A test unit, to be named Sturmstaffel 1, was established in October/November 1943. Göring visited the unit on November 17, 1943 at Achmer. Kornatzki himself had travelled Germany to interview volunteer pilots, impressing on these men his views and concepts of this new type of air warfare. Of course, for most Luftwaffe pilots, the prospect of volunteering for the Sturmstaffel held no appeal whatsoever—expectations of these new aerial shock troops were high, and the volunteers were left in no doubt of the dangers they would face and the chilling fact that many of them would not survive. Early volunteers—no doubt full of youthful enthusiasm or fanaticism—were required to sign an oath affirming that they would shoot down at least one bomber per mission and pledging their commitment to bring the enemy down by ramming in midair if necessary. Each of the pilots signed the following document in a simple ceremony:

> I have volunteered for the Sturmstaffel of my own free will. I fully understand the fundamental principles of the Staffel.
>
> 1. ALL ATTACKS WILL, WITHOUT EXCEPTION, BE CARRIED OUT IN FORMATION AND TO WITHIN THE CLOSEST POSSIBLE RANGE OF THE ENEMY.
>
> 2. LOSSES SUFFERED DURING THE APPROACH WILL BE COMPENSATED FOR BY IMMEDIATELY CLOSING UP ON THE FORMATION LEADER.
>
> 3. THE ENEMY UNDER ATTACK IS TO BE SHOT DOWN FROM THE SHORTEST RANGE POSSIBLE OR, IF THIS IS UNSUCCESSFUL, DESTROYED BY RAMMING.
>
> 4. THE STURM PILOT WILL REMAIN IN CONTACT WITH THE STRICKEN ENEMY UNTIL THE POINT OF IMPACT WITH THE GROUND HAS BEEN ESTABLISHED.
>
> I voluntarily accept the obligation to abide by these principles, and I will not return to base without having destroyed my enemy. Should I violate these principles, I am prepared to face court martial or dismissal from the Staffel.

Oskar Bösch was just one of the Sturmstaffel's new recruits. Asked decades later about the Sturmstaffel's ramming mission he recalled:

> Our duty, if we couldn't shoot the bomber down through cannon fire, was to bring it down by ramming it, using our propellers like giant circular saws to hack through the tailplane. I remember on one sortie suddenly there was a bomber in front of me, and I was out of ammunition and the opportunity was there to fly a ramming attack. I was about 50 meters behind the bomber and caught in the turbulent slipstream from the engines … it was all I could do to keep my aircraft under control. I was buffeted about and then literally tossed over the Boeing's wing, missing it by about half a meter with my wing.

Fw 190 A-6 White 9 was flown by Fw. Otto Weissenberger, younger brother of Hptm. Theo Weissenberger, the leading *Experte* of JG 5. Otto was shot down and killed in this machine on March 23, 1944 over Nordick. Note the antenna mast for the FuG 16ZY under the port wing.

Fw 190 A-6 of Sturmstaffel 1 having its engine run-up. Note the unit emblem on the engine cowl: an armored fist clutching a bolt of lightning. The black-white-black RVT bands can be seen around the rear fuselage.

Sturmstaffel 1 pilots line up for a final photo prior to their unit being incorporated into IV./JG 3 under Kommandeur Hptm. Wilhelm Moritz, late April 1944. Unit commander Maj. Hans-Günther von Kornatzki is fifth from left. To his left is Lt. Werner Gerth, awarded the Knight's Cross for some 26 victories in late October 1944; he was killed just days later. Fourth right is Uffz. Willi Maximowitz, another successful ace in the defense of the Reich. Uffz. Oskar Bösch is second from the right. Other aces in the unit included Lt. Richard Franz, Ofw. Wolfgang Kosse, Lt. Siegfried Müller (third from the left) who survived the war as Staffelkapitän 13./JG 3 with 17 victories, and Lt. Rudolf Metz (fourth from left), killed on October 6, 1944 with around ten victories.

Gefechtsbericht (combat report) February 21, 1944: Hans Weik, 10./JG 3

On 21.2.44 at 12:40 I took off with 12 Bf 109s to intercept enemy formations heading toward Hanover. Over Rothenburg we rendezvoused and assembled with two other Gruppen. At 13:25 at 8,000 meters we sighted the enemy formation ... At 14:43 we flew a head-on pass against a formation of some 40 Fortress IIs. I flew on the right-hand side directly behind Oblt. Kutscha. At a range of about 400 meters I found myself in a very good firing position directly in front. I achieved hits in the starboard wing and in the fuselage and observed parts flying off. Pulling up, I lost sight of Oblt. Kutscha who had to land because of lack of fuel ... I then repeated my attack from the same position on the right side and scored hits in the rear of the fuselage. Following this pass, I had to break off as I was running low on fuel. I could see the shot-up aircraft trailing a light plume of smoke, losing height and dropping out of the formation.

Staffelkapitän of 6./JG 27, who six months earlier had fought over Sicily. He became disorientated in the clouds after combat and subsequently crashed near Würrisch/Hunsrück, Germany. He had scored 53 victories, including 20 heavy bombers. On July 20, 1944—the day of the failed assassination attempt on Hitler—he was posthumously awarded the Oak Leaves to his Knight's Cross.

On February 20, 1944 the USAAF mounted their biggest raid of the war to date, launching more than a thousand B-17s and B-24s to open *Big Week*, a concerted campaign against aircraft manufacturing plants, targeting Oschersleben, Leipzig, Tutow, and Braunschweig. IV./JG 3 and its eager young *Jagdflieger*—men like Lt. Hans Weik—found themselves in the front line. After serving in the East, Lt. Hans Weik flew as a fighter pilot instructor with 4./Ergänzungs-Jagdgruppe Ost. However, his duties as an instructor did not preclude combat, for on September 6, 1943, he downed his first four-engined bomber, a USAAF B-17 raiding Stuttgart. In November 1943, he was transfered to 9./JG 3 based at Bad Wörishofen. On February 19, 1944, Weik was appointed Staffelkapitän of 10./JG 3 after the death in action of Oblt. Alfred Humer (21 victories). Based in the Netherlands, IV./JG 3 was scrambled from Venlo on February 21 against waves of incoming B-17s. Weik downed one over Holzminden.

Despite this success, IV./JG 3's results for February were mediocre—no more than three kills, and four HSS for 23 Bf 109s brought down and 13 pilots killed, including the Gruppenkommandeur Maj. Franz Beyer on February 11. March saw seven *Einsatztage*, while April witnessed 12 combat days under new Kommandeur Friedrich-Karl Müller. Based at Salzwedel during April 1944, IV./JG 3 flew sorties in concert with the Sturmstaffel and enjoyed a measure of success—no fewer than 53 *Viermots* and 38 HSS. Late on April 24, Weik bailed out unharmed in combat as IV./JG 3 was scrambled at 18:20 against B-24s attacking western areas of the Reich. During this engagement new Kommandeur Hptm. Moritz achieved his first victory with IV./JG 3, Maj. F-K. Müller having been appointed Kommodore of JG 3. Between February and April 1944, Weik, flying his usual Bf 109 G-6 White 7 as Staffelkapitän 10./JG 3, shot down a number of *Viermots*. Also on the IV./JG 3 pilot roster were young *Jagdflieger* such as Willi Unger and Hans Iffland. Unger did not make his first combat sortie until late March 1944 but during April shot down eight heavy bombers. Hans Iffland had some 16 heavy bomber kills during this period, including one of the 13 bombers claimed by the unit on the March 6 Berlin raid, one of the costliest ever mounted by the Eighth Air Force. All three would survive the war and both Weik and Unger would go on to earn the Knight's Cross.

In a visit on April 15, 1944 General der Jagdflieger Galland announced that IV./JG 3 was to adopt the *Sturm* role along the lines of the Sturmstaffel, the unit alongside which they were based and which would now be incorporated into IV./JG 3. The Sturmstaffel flew the *Sturmbock* (battering ram) Focke Wulf 190; heavily armed with cannon, well protected with a reinforced canopy and side armor, the *Sturmbock* 190s were able to close from the rear, absorbing the defensive fire from the bomber combat boxes and only opening up when assured of a kill. IV./JG 3 based at Salzwedel was the first *Sturm* unit to fly in Gruppe strength. In early May Hans Weik and his comrades in IV./JG 3 started flight conversion and training on the Focke-Wulf 190, as Weik recalled in one of the last interviews he gave before his death in 2001:

> I made my first solo flight in the Focke-Wulf 190 on May 2, 1944 and trained until June 27 when we were granted a period of rest which lasted until July 6. All the Focke-Wulfs assigned to our unit were brand-new machines and in just about all respects could not really be compared to the 109s that we had flown previously. The Focke-Wulf 190 was a considerably stronger and more robust machine. I found the heavily armed and armored A-8/R2 variant somewhat difficult to fly, but thanks to its air-cooled radial engine, it proved relatively trouble-free. We *Sturmgruppe* pilots were of course primarily concerned with armor and armament, rather than a kilometer or more of top speed. Our Fw 190s mounted extremely effective armament due to the special ammunition—our *Minengranten* [mine shells] exploded on contact when they slammed into a bomber. However, unleashing a burst of fire from the Mk 108 cannon made the Focke-Wulf extremely unstable. Armor was important for us—since we were only some 70–90 kph faster than the bombers, our overtaking speed was slow, which meant that we spent a long time in their defensive fire zone. This required steely nerves.

Staffelkapitän 10./JG 3, Lt. Hans Weik made only 85 *Feindflüge* and returned 36 victories, including 22 four-engined bombers. He was awarded the Knights Cross on July 27, 1944. Attacking B-17s raiding Memmingen on July 18, 1944, he was wounded by return fire while flying Fw 190A-8/R2 (W.Nr. 680747) White 7. His wounds were serious enough to keep him from further front-line duties.

Willi Unger in the cockpit of his Fw 190, late 1944. In August, he received the German Cross in Gold and promotion to Oberfeldwebel. By September 1944, he had transferred to 15.(Sturm)/JG 3, and was awarded the Knight's Cross on October 23 for 19 heavy bomber victories.

On April 29, 1944, some 679 USAAF bombers formed up over southern England for a mission to Berlin. Sturmstaffel 1 was airborne shortly after 10:00. Joining up with IV./JG 3 (led in the air by Lt. Hans Weik), an impressive *Gefechtsverband* (battle formation) assembled over Magdeburg and headed out in the direction of Braunschweig, making visual contact with the incoming bombers at 11:00. Northeast of Braunschweig the Stumstaffel was to carry out one of the most successful *Sturm* assaults in its short history, attacking a force of some 40 bombers detached from the main force. In less than half an hour almost half of them had been hacked down. Oskar Bösch recalled:

> I was airborne at 10 a.m. and flew as wingman to Lt. Werner Gerth who was leading our flight of more than a dozen Fw 190s. An hour later we found what we were looking for—more than 40 Flying Fortresses … we assumed our *Angriffskeil* arrowhead attack formation in line abreast behind them. From more than half a mile away I saw the muzzle flashes from their defensive fire. Picking out a bomber, I let its wings grow larger in my gunsight, my finger resting on the firing button. That's when I was hit. The first impact shocked me, the second and third tore off the canopy. The cacophony and intense cold of the slipstream assailed my senses. I closed on the B-17 and let him have it from all barrels. All around me there were explosions and tracers as my comrades tore into the formation. I didn't have time

Uffz. Willi Maximowitz standing on the wing of White 2, a Sturmstaffel machine flown by Uffz. Gerd Vivroux (here seated on the cockpit sill). Note the armored glass "blinkers" attached to the canopy.

to think about living or dying—I was just focused on shooting the bomber down. Fire began to spread over the B-17's wing and it corkscrewed down out of control.

Uffz. Willi Maximowitz was another successful Sturmstaffel pilot, claiming a B-17 shot down over Helmstedt. He had already achieved his first success when he shot down a USAAF B-24 on January 30, 1944. On March 23, 1944, Maximowitz was credited with a successful *Rammabschuss* (a downing by ramming) when he collided with a 92nd Bombardment Group B-17 raiding Braunschweig in north-central Germany. His heavily damaged Focke-Wulf 190 A-6 (W.Nr. 551099) White 10 was hosed by the bombers' defensive fire and a wounded Maximowitz had to bail out near Wuppertal. This was one of only two ramming attacks recorded during the brief five-month existence of the Sturmstaffel. The B-17 Fortress that he tangled with managed to return to England despite missing a section of horizontal stabilizer.

Barely a week after the April 29, 1944 raid, Oskar Bösch was credited with an *Herausschuss*, as over 700 USAAF bombers screened by a similar number of escorts again raided Berlin and Braunschweig. "I clearly remember the May 8 mission which went wrong from the beginning. Our own Flak unwittingly used us for target practice and my aircraft was riddled with shrapnel."

On May 8, 1944 Sturmstaffel 1 was redesignated as 11. Staffel of IV./JG 3 under new Gruppenkommandeur Hptm. Willi Moritz. IV./JG 3 was re-equipped with the Fw 190. The Sturmstaffel experiment had patently enjoyed a measure of success. All told some 62 heavy bombers had been claimed shot down between 11 January and 29 April 1944, for the loss of 11 of the original pilot complement killed in action. Their actions heralded a more general expansion of units using these methods with both II./JG 300 and II./JG 4 converting to the *Sturm* role during the summer of 1944. However, it would prove to be far too little and far too late for the Luftwaffe. Less than a month later, on June 6, the D-Day landings in Normandy saw the focus of the Luftwaffe's defensive effort urgently switch to France. And from its bases in Italy the USAAF Fifteenth Air Force carried out no fewer than 18 large-scale raids on Germany during July 1944 alone.

Leading pilots continued to fall. On February 25, Hptm. Josef Haiböck, leading I./JG 3 and with 77 victories, was killed near Karlsruhe. He was able to land but his aircraft was then machine-gunned by USAAF fighters.

Field Marshal Erwin Rommel, with Kommodore Priller, reviews III./JG 26 still equipped with the Bf 109. The Allied "invasion" was expected soon.

On March 2, another exceptional veteran, Obstlt. Egon Mayer, leading JG 2, was killed in action. Airborne with his Geschwaderstab from Cormeilles, northeast of Lisieux, Normandy, Kommodore Mayer—the "ace of aces" in the West—was vectored over the Ardennes against a USAAF daylight raid aimed at Frankfurt am Main. Mayer was flying with a new Schwarm having suffered the recent loss of his long-time wingmen, Gruppenadjutant Hptm. Fritz Edelmann (killed January 30) and Ofw. Rudolf Alf (hospitalized January 21). All four Fw 190s missed the rendezvous with II. Gruppe, airborne from Creil, north of Paris, and III. Gruppe, which had overnighted at St. Trond, Belgium. Continuing northeastward, Mayer appears to have subsequently lost the other three Fw 190s of his Schwarm and, as an "isolated Fw 190," he was easily picked off by 365th Fighter Group P-47 Thunderbolts near Montmédy (a first victory for Maj. Robert L. Goffey). He was the third Kommodore of the Richthofener to be shot down and killed after Wick and Balthasar. His award of the Swords was announced on the day of his death. Egon Mayer had filed claims for some 102 enemy aircraft, all in the West, including 26 four-engined bombers, 51 Spitfires and 12 P-47 fighters. His funeral was held at Beaumont with much pomp and ceremony. In his guard of honor were Huppertz and Wurmheller, both of whom would meet a similar fate.

On March 8, Obfw. Rudolf Ehrenberger, attached to II./JG 53 since 1940 and a successful ace over Malta and Sicily, was shot down near Wittemberg. Flying RVT duties from bases in Germany, Ehrenberger had returned six victories including three USAAF B-24s shot down on February 25, 1944. On March 8, 1944, Ehrenberger engaged USAAF bombers and fighters near Wittemberg. In the resulting action his Bf 109 G-6 (W.Nr. 440111) took hits. He bailed out but was then shot and killed in his parachute. Ehrenberger was posthumously awarded the Knight's Cross on April 5, having been credited with 49 victories. On March 23, Obest Wolf-Dietrich "Fürst" Wilcke, another important figure in the Tagjagd, leading JG 3, was killed in combat near Schöppenstedt. He had received the Oak Leaves for his 162 victories and, at the beginning of the year, had asked to return to combat despite a flight ban.

On April 8, Lt. Karl Willius, a 1940 veteran flying in 2./JG 26, was shot down over the Zuiderzee, Netherlands, after downing a B-24. He would receive the Knight's Cross posthumously for his 50 *Luftsiege*. Also on April 8, Staffelkapitän of 1./JG 11, Oblt. Josef "Jupp" Zwernemann, was set upon by a dozen Mustangs near Gardelegen and bailed out, only to be strafed in his parachute. He had downed a Liberator and a P-51 for his 125th and 126th kills. Prior to serving in the defense of the Reich, he had been one of the most successful pilots of 9./JG 52. In October 1942, having scored his 103rd kill, he was awarded the Oak Leaves to his Knight's Cross.

On April 9, III./JG 54 was scrambled against large bomber formations, intercepting them over Kiel. Among the pilots downed over Schleswig-Holstein were Uffz. Günther Sahl in his Bf 109 G-6 Black 8 (W.Nr. 26048) and 7./JG 54 Staffelkapitän Oblt. Rudolf Klemm in his G-6 White 1 with *Gondelwaffen*—the underslung MG 151s. Klemm had accumulated 32 victories at the time. In total III./ JG 54 lost seven Bf 109s for one P-47 claimed. Klemm returned to the Eastern Front with JG 54 later that summer.

On May 11, the talented Obstlt. Walter Oesau, JG 1 Kommodore, was shot down over St. Vith. He had 127 *Abschüsse* to his credit (including ten in Spain and 14 four-engined

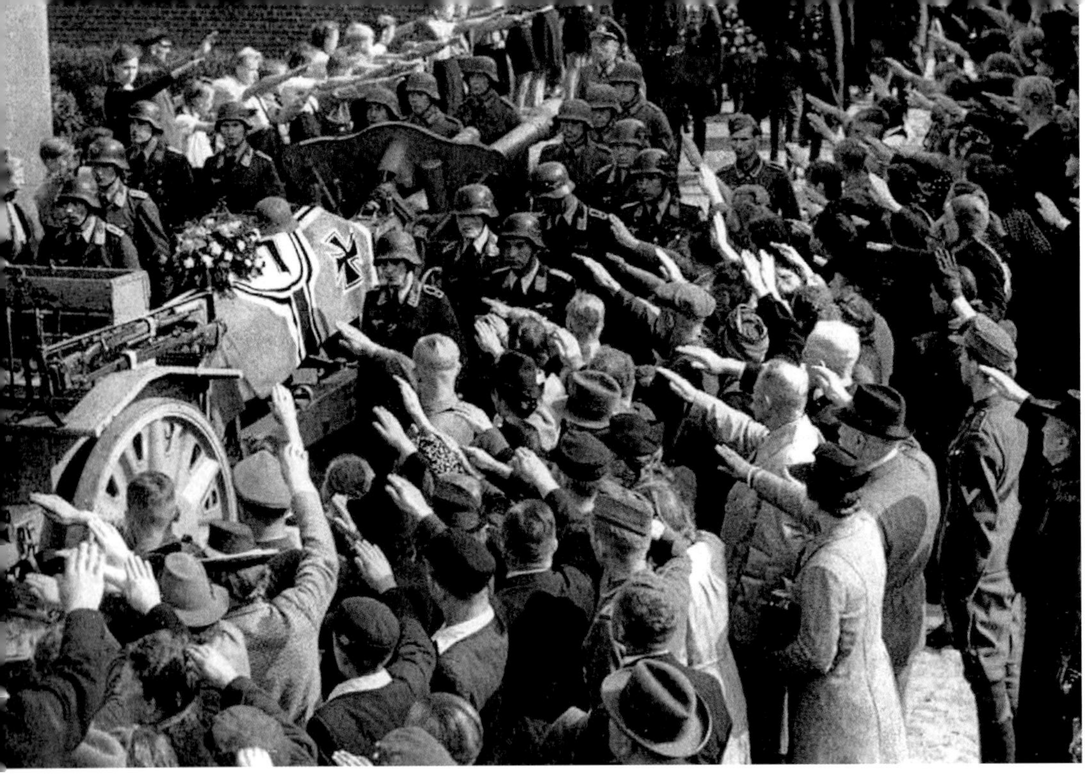

Obstlt. Walter Oesau was buried at Melsungen. Large crowds turned out to salute the fallen Kommodore, as his coffin was transported through the town on a gun carriage decorated with flowers.

bombers) and was one of the leading Luftwaffe fighter aces and commanders at the time of his death. Oesau's death has often been portrayed in a variety of often purely speculative accounts. What is known is that Oesau was airborne from Paderborn with his wingman, Lt. Rudolf Schnappauf, during the early evening of May 11, 1944 to intercept Allied bombers raiding northeastern Belgium and Luxembourg. According to various U.S. accounts he was bounced by up to five escorting P-38s of the 474th FG—or perhaps P-51s of 354th FG—and chased from high altitude down to the deck. Robert Skawran in his account notes that Oesau was on his own by this stage; Schnappauf had been wounded at the start of the encounter and his machine had sustained damage. Ordered to break off, he had dropped away. The

Kommodore JG 2, Maj. Kurt Ubben—appointed as successor to Egon Mayer on March 2, 1944—is about to climb out of his FW 190 A-8. He had flown with JG 77 in Norway, Russia, and the Mediterranean. However, before he could adapt to the fighting on this new front, he was shot down and killed on April 27, 1944, possibly in this FW 190 A-8 (W.Nr. 680113) <<—+—. He attempted to bail out at low altitude but his 'chute failed to fully deploy.

Lightnings took it in turns to put in firing passes: two machines attacking, others waiting at a slightly higher altitude to take over. The fight had lasted almost 20 minutes when Oesau's Bf 109 was hit and crippled. Oesau attempted to make an emergency landing and was shot down just above the ground. His lifeless body was found in the vicinity of his burned-out Bf 109 with several bullet wounds, presumed shot dead before his aircraft hit the ground.

Heavily outnumbered, the tenacity of the Luftwaffe pilots was no longer sufficient to defend the skies of the occupied territories, especially France. Every sortie—or so it appeared—was a massacre of both "old hands" and "new growth" alike. Pilots and aircraft were shot down almost at will by superior numbers of U.S. fighters. In the months and weeks prior to D-Day the Allied bombing and interdiction campaign over France reached its height.

On May 24, as 2nd Bombardment Division B-24s carpet-bombed airfields in France, 616 Fortresses of the 1st and 3rd BDs escorted by over 900 fighters headed for Berlin, crossing the coast from the north over Schleswig-Holstein. Some 14 Tagjagd Gruppen were directed against this raid, including Fw 190 pilot Fritz Engau's I./JG 11:

> it was one of the most notable sorties I flew as a day fighter. We could only fly the occasional mission in the kind of poor visibility we met that day. We were about ten Fw 190s and we flew in an arrowhead formation. We managed to turn into a box of two or three *Pulks*—each of 18 bombers—but were not quite correctly lined up on them. With Oblt. Hans-Heinrich Koenig leading, we headed toward the formation all guns blazing. Suddenly there was a flash. Koenig had failed to pull up in time and had smashed full tilt into a B-17. The bright explosion was probably his explosive rounds going off. I saw huge pieces of debris spinning away. As we passed through the *Pulk* and swept into a turn to fly a second pass, there was no sign of the B-17 that had been hit. But I could still see the wreck of Koenig's machine tumbling down, wings torn off. It was not burning … but there was no parachute.

At the time of his death "King" Koenig was one of the most experienced, and with 28 victories including 20 *Viermots*, one of the most successful formation leaders in the day fighter force defending the Reich. His performance was all the more noteworthy for having lost an eye when flying as a night fighter and, according to Engau, it was this sight defect in such poor weather that accounted for his collision. He was posthumously promoted to Hauptmann and on August 19 awarded the Knight's Cross.

On May 25, 1944, over 1,000 Eighth Air Force bombers escorted by 811 fighters set out to target rail hubs and infrastructure in northeastern France and the Saarland region of western Germany, as well as coastal defenses along the Channel. Ofhr. Hubert Heckmann of 9./JG 1 had overslept and, having missed the bus pickup, had to walk some five kilometers to the airfield at Störmede, where his Gruppe was at cockpit readiness:

> When I got to the airfield the Gruppe was already at *Sitzbereitschaft*. I managed to grab a couple of slices of bread from the breakfast table and while I was being strapped into Yellow 15, our orderly Meier arrived with a fried egg to put between them. Once the Gruppe was airborne, we assembled over the field and headed south—some 20 machines. At 8,000 meters altitude it was a clear sunny day. After a while we could see the Alps in the distance. We received instructions from

> the ground to turn around and head back to Herzogenaurach and land there … everything happened so quickly from that point. A line of P-51s was heading toward us … that was when I realized I was on my own. At the same time, I saw a puff of smoke on the ground and heard, "I've got one" in my headset. I curved around to the north, watching my back all the while and saw another machine off to my left, some way distant. It was a Mustang. I had folded the Revi [gunsight] back, expecting to land soon but now I had the time to swing it out into my line of sight, line up on him and give him a burst. Before I could see any impacts, my weapon jammed. Barely two or three rounds fired and I was now no more than five meters behind him: no question of pulling up or away to one side. I was a sitting duck! *Rammstoss!*

Having passed over the village of Botenheim, Heckmann's Bf 109 G-6/AS had come up behind Capt. Joseph H. Bennett's P-51 B-5 Mustang (43-6572, "VF–N Paul"), while staying below the P-51's propwash. With his guns jammed, Heckmann pulled up to the P-51's height and rammed his Bf 109 right into the tail of Bennett's aircraft. The impact sheared off the tail and rear fuselage section of the Mustang. With his aircraft's nose thrust skyward, Bennett bailed out near Botenheim. His own aircraft seriously damaged, Heckmann pulled off a successful belly-landing. Bennett, a former Eagle Squadron RAF pilot, was captured. Heckmann later came to introduce himself and meet the pilot of his first victory.

The losses being sustained against the USAAF meant increasing numbers of new and poorly trained replacement pilots were arriving in front-line units. According to a veteran of III./JG 77:

> towards the end of the war we had very little contact with the new pilots that were arriving at the unit. We *alte Hase* [old hares] kept to ourselves and hardly spoke to the *Nachwuchs* [newcomers]. Why? Their life expectancy at the time was limited to no more than a handful of combat flights. If we got to know them and they were subsequently killed a few sorties later as was likely, then this could be very upsetting.

The veterans employed certain "tricks" to survive. According to a member of JG 1:

> When we had to take off in an emergency to fight Fortresses, I would quickly find small aerodromes on the map of the area. After the engagement, I would try to land on one of them. The personnel there were delighted to receive a combat aviator and, as most often, there was no special gasoline [high octane aviation fuel] for fighters, I could relax for a day or two while being well fed, waiting for the gas to arrive. When I returned to the *Kasino* [officers' mess], I noticed the disappearance of comrades and the new faces who had arrived to replace them.

With the invasion of the Continent looming and the Reich being pounded almost daily by massive bombing raids, even JG 5—the *Eismeer* Geschwader fighting in the Far North—was transferred back to Europe, I. and II./JG 5 transferring in late May 1944 from the Artic Circle to southern Germany. Here they re-equipped with new Bf 109 G-6 fighters. In June 1944, both Gruppen deployed to France to oppose the Allied landings.

Normandy and the Invasion of France, 1944

On D-Day, June 6, 1944, the Allies landed in Normandy. Fighter Gruppen were urgently dispatched from Germany to reinforce JG 2 and 26 already present in France. Compared to the 15,000 sorties flown by Allied aircraft on D-Day itself, the Luftwaffe only flew around 300; four days later no fewer than 1,300 Luftwaffe machines, including nearly 500 fighters belonging to some 20 fighter Gruppen were able to mount combat sorties. Well informed by Ultra however, Allied bombers hunted down the JGs on their airfields. Despite this total enemy superiority, a handful of notably talented pilots were able to make their presence felt.

At noon on June 6, 1944, Obstlt. Kurt Bühligen (who would return his 100th kill the next day) and Hptm. Hubert Huppertz of III./JG 2 were flying two of the 29 Fw 190s that attacked at least 24 Thunderbolts of the U.S. 365th FG and Typhoons of 183 Sqn RAF. The Germans claimed six Allied fighters downed—including two Typhoons in less than two minutes by

Kommandeur I./JG 5 Weissenberger at cockpit readiness in his Gustav; note the refined cowl shape of his Bf 109, possibly a G-6/AS variant. He had replaced Maj. Horst Carganico—shot down and killed on May 27, 1944—as Kommandeur I./JG 5 on June 4, 1944. He was awarded the Knight's Cross on November 13, 1942 after 38 kills. The Oak Leaves were awarded on August 2, 1943 after 112 victories. He survived the war with a total of 208 victories, a number of them on Me 262s with JG 7.

Many aces perished in Normandy, including the high-scorers brought back from the East. On June 7, Hptm. Karl-Heinz Weber, leading III./JG 1, was reported missing in his Bf 109 south of Rouen—his first sortie in the West. His 136 victories had all been returned in the East with 7./JG 51. He was posthumously awarded the Oak Leaves.

Huppertz—for a single loss. Actual Allied losses in this engagement were five (two P-47s, three Typhoons). That same evening, Huppertz caught eight Typhoons of 164 Sqn and shot down one. In the course of another sortie late on June 6, Huppertz engaged the numerically superior formations of Allied aircraft, which by that time filled the skies. During this single mission, Huppertz was entangled in combat with several Allied fighter units, involving both Mustangs and Thunderbolts, but in spite of the odds he claimed a Mustang and a Thunderbolt to total five victories—ace in a day. Just two days later he was killed in action. At 09:15, III./JG 2 was airborne with around ten machines and engaged by Mustangs and possibly Thunderbolts around Caen. Hptm. Wurmheller claimed one Mustang, while three Fw 190s were shot down; two of the JG 2 pilots were killed, including Gruppenkommandeur Huppertz.

On the same day, elements of Hptm. Theo Weissenberger's I./JG 5 arrived on the "invasion front" at Montdidier in the vicinity of the French capital. Weissenberger himself and the rest of his Gruppe clashed with P-47s coming into Montdidier

Hptm. Herbert Huppertz led III./JG 2 into action on June 6, 1944. Having claimed his first victory, a Spitfire, over Dunkirk on May 28, 1940 with 6./JG 51, his tally at the start of June 1944 was around 70 confirmed. He claimed five kills on June 6 but was shot down and killed two days later over Caen. He was posthumously awarded the Oak Leaves.

Despite heavy losses, the *Experten* did win victories over Normandy. Being feted here is JG 26 Kommodore Priller's 100th *Luftsieg*, achieved on June 15, 1944 over a B-24 near Dreux. The award of the Swords followed soon afterward.

Priller in one of the many Fw 190s that he flew marked Black 13 and displaying the *Jutta* playing card.

Flying Fw 190 A-8 (W.Nr. 170736), Lt. Eugen-Ludwig Zweigart of III./JG 54 was shot down and killed near Les Champeaux, southwest of Vimoutiers, Normandy, on June 8, 1944. He bailed out but was strafed in his parachute, Aged 30, he was credited with 69 victories.

on June 7. I./JG 5 also saw combat over Beauvais that same day; in total Weissenberger claimed five victories. He filed a further three claims the following day. On June 8, 1944 he was interviewed by a *Kriegsberichter*, a war reporter, with Oblt. Lothar Gerlach, Staffelkapitän of 1./JG 5. Weissenberger went on to return his 199th and 200th victories on July 25, and with some 25 victories was by some distance the most successful Jagdwaffe pilot over Normandy. While some of his "invasion victories" cannot be confirmed from Allied records, overall his success would have little impact and, after a few weeks of fighting, the Wehrmacht was in headlong retreat eastward.

The fighter units continue to lose pilots and *Experten*. On June 22, U.S. VII Corps commander, General "Lightning Joe" Collins, launched his final assault on von Schlieben's 21,000 men cut off in the port of Cherbourg. The Richthofener flew several morning sorties and during the afternoon brought together the remnants of II and III. Gruppen for a joint sortie of around 20 machines (II. Gruppe flying out of Baron had only a handful of serviceable Fw 190s). Lt. Paul Müngersdorff, Staffelführer of 5./JG 2, flew the sortie:

> reinforced with machines from III. Gruppe, we took off to attack enemy positions. Reaching a height of 6,000 meters, we headed in the direction of Normandy. We

III./JG 26 Bf 109 Gustavs taxiing out for takeoff at Villacoublay, Paris, June 1944.

Lt. Karl-Heinz Kempf of JG 26 was a former Green Heart Geschwader pilot with 65 victories over the course of some 400 sorties by the time of the Normandy invasion. He was awarded the Knight's Cross in Russia during 1942, based at Villacoublay with 9./JG 26,

Bf 109 G-6 flown by Lt. Hans-Ulrich Jung, Staffelkapitän 10./JG 3, being wheeled out of cover in June/July 1944. Jung crashed to his death on January 1, 1945.

> never got there. U.S. fighters were waiting for us over Lisieux. We immediately jettisoned our drop tanks and a huge swirling dogfight developed over a large area of the sky against a largely numerically superior enemy. I had the devil of a job getting out unscathed. Banking into one turn, I caught sight of Wurmheller's machine curving away to the west. Just then he plunged into a dive but seemed to have been hit by a burst of fire. I was convinced he had been killed outright at that same moment since he made no attempt to pull up and plummeted into the ground. After landing I called up the Stab and informed them myself that Wurmheller had been killed in action.

Lt. Christoph Dezius, Staffelführer of 7./JG 2, recalled:

> our Gruppe having shrunk to virtually nothing, we were deployed in concert with III. Gruppe under Hptm. Wurmheller. As we were heading toward Saint-Lô, we were surprised on the bounce by a squadron of P-51s that none of us had spotted. They dove on us with a height advantage of some 30 meters. Wurmheller was hit as he threw his crate into a turn. A Mustang had latched onto his tail.

On August 6, Lt. August Mors (6./JG 5) was shot down near Beaumont. He bailed out but his 'chute caught up on a tree. He died in Clichy hospital some two days later. Mors had shot down 48 Soviet machines and, during his short spell of combat in the West, claimed a further 12 victories. He was awarded the Knight's Cross posthumously.

With the shift to Normandy and the invasion front, only some ten Jagdgruppen were left defending the Reich through June and July 1944. Of these the most potent force were the three Gruppen of JG 300. A single-seat night-fighter Wilde Sau (Wild Boar) Geschwader, a Gruppen of JG 300 was undergoing conversion training to the day fighter role during May and June 1944 under Major Walther Dahl, now appointed Kommodore. As the day fighter arm of the Luftwaffe was essentially a "fair-weather" force, the Wilde Sau had been deployed

Lt. Hans-Ulrich Jung of III./JG 3 (left). Note the German Cross in Gold on his flying jacket. Jung was posted to III./JG 3 from IV.(Sturm)./JG 3 when the Sturmgruppe departed France after only a couple of days at the front during late June 1944.

Bf 109 G-6 flown by Hptm. Gerhard Stamp, Gruppenkommandeur I./JG 300. Stamp had won the Knight's Cross with LG 1 at the controls of a Ju 88 bomber.

on day fighter sorties as early as December 1943—Eighth Air Force raids mounted in poor weather conditions could only be countered by these instrument-qualified pilots.

The cadre of battle-hardened pilots in I. and II./JG 300 included Knight's Cross bearer Hptm. Gerd Stamp, a successful Ju 88 bomber pilot with LG 1, while Hubert Engst and Lt. Gerhard Bärsdorf had both scored their first *Viermot* victories over the infernos of Hamburg back in July 1943 as Wilde Sau night fighters. Konrad Bauer, an Eastern Front ace with JG 51, would go on to become the leading Fw 190 ace in the defense of the Reich during the summer of 1944 with II./ JG 300. His comrade Lt. Klaus Bretschneider had already claimed 14 night kills in just 20 Wilde Sau sorties flying a Neptun-gerät radar-equipped Fw 190 from Rheine during the early months of 1944 and was one of the best-known *Sturm* pilots during the summer of 1944.

On June 29, 1944 over 1,000 Eighth Air Force bombers escorted by over 600 fighters raided the synthetic oil plant at Böhlen. Directed to oppose this vast force in the region of Leipzig were just 23 Bf 109s from I./JG 300 which had been scrambled from Herzogenaurach near Erlangen with perhaps a similar number of Fw 190s of II./JG 300, some pilots flying their first daylight combat sorties. Bounced by P-51s, Hptm. Gerhard Stamp, Gruppenkommandeur I./JG 300, was shot down and wounded along with six other pilots from his Gruppe. Despite drawing off the escort, thus enabling pilots of II./JG 300 to carry out *Sturm*-type attacks on a B-17 and a B-24 box—Oblt. Ernst-Erich Hirschfeld of 6. Staffel claimed a B-24 near Eisleben for his 18th victory—a number of highly experienced former II. Gruppe night fighters were shot down including the Gruppenkommandeur, Kurd Peters.

USAAF escort fighters were increasingly effective against the German fighters laden as they were with heavy weapons. JG 300 lost several of its top aces during the summer of 1944. On July 28, 1944, Oblt. Ernst-Erich Hirschfeld (24 kills, nine at night) of 5./JG 300 was shot down and killed in his Fw 190 A-8 near Erfurt, as was Lt. Gerhard Bärsdorf (seven kills) who collided with his wingman. On July 29, 1944, Obfw. Hermann Wischnewski (26 kills) of I./JG 300 shot down two B-17s and a P-51 but was in turn shot down and badly injured.

Kurt Gabler was a Wilde Sau ace and achieved some 17 day and night victories returned in only 23 combat sorties. This is Bf 109 G-6 Red 8 of 8./JG 300. Gabler was wounded during the Arnhem operation of late September 1944 as Staffelkapitän 11./JG 300, and sidelined for the rest of the war.

On July 18, 1944, III./ JG 300's Kurt Gabler—airborne from Jüterbog—became the first Luftwaffe pilot to shoot down an RAF Mosquito over Berlin by day.

> We were ordered to put 109s in the air to hunt Mosquitos between Magdeburg and Berlin. I lifted off at 11:30 with the Kapitän of 9. Staffel, Oblt. Gottuck, as wingman. We were excellently guided by our radar to a height of 11,500 meters over Berlin. I then spotted a Mosquito flying five kilometers ahead of me. Despite activating my engine's methanol injection, I was unable to reel him in. I gained barely several hundred meters on him … and watched as my oil temperature approached its critical level. Suddenly, while heading eastward away from Berlin, the Englishman curved into a wide starboard sweep. I had difficulty staying calm: up until then no Mosquito had fallen to the guns of a Luftwaffe day fighter over Berlin ... In front of me the Mosquito tightened his turn. In turn I hauled my ship brutally into a curve to the right. The fact that I was trailing was no longer a handicap, it was going to allow me to pick him off as he came out of his turn. The enemy crew must have been unaware of my presence otherwise they would never have carried out such a suicidal maneuver. The Mosquito came out of his 180° turn at an altitude of 11,300 meters. I did likewise and came in behind him to within firing range. Had he spotted me at that moment, it would have been easy for him to evade me. But it was not to be. My first burst struck home. His starboard engine immediately erupted in flames. I saw the two-man crew bail out. The Mosquito, now ablaze like a torch, went down near Zerbst. My third aerial victory of the day—and what a victory! Gottuck was the first to congratulate me over the radio. You can imagine how happy I and my comrades were as I touched down at 13:05 at Jüterbog. Incidentally, I'm still waiting for the case of champagne famously promised by Göring to any pilot shooting down a Mosquito over Berlin.

On July 21, 1944, the Eighth and Fifteenth U.S. Air Forces targeted ball-bearing plants, aeronautical industries, and airfields in southwest Germany and a synthetic oil refinery in Czechoslovakia. A total of 1,497 bombers were assembled and dispatched in six formations, headed for Munich, Kottern/Kempten, Regensburg/Obertraubling, Prüfening, Ebelsbach, Schweinfurt, and Brüx, screened by an escort of 1,124 fighters.

Seventeen III./JG 300 Bf 109s were airborne by 09:15 from Jüterbog, led off by a 109 displaying a single chevron and flown by Oblt. Kurt Gabler. They climbed in the direction of the Alps south of Munich. Gabler leveled out at 8,000 meters. Formed up in Schwärme, the Messerschmitts tore into a formation of 100–120 Liberators of the 2nd BD. Kurt Gabler recalled:

> Hardly had the enemy been identified when I gave the order to jettison auxiliary tanks and switch on gunsights. The first American parachutes appeared. Our assault was devastating. Everything happened in just a few seconds. Everyone was concentrating on his target and our ships shook to the rhythm of salvos of 2-cm shells. I knocked down a B-24, which plummeted earthward in flames, and slid in quickly toward a second. As it attempted to flee to Switzerland, my salvos struck home several times. Pieces of debris flew off and then it began to plunge down out of control toward the Alps. I saw it catch fire. The American gunners had returned fire in equal measure, seriously damaging my 109. My attention was suddenly drawn to the smoke seeping into the cockpit. My Messerschmitt was also burning! I parted company at 7,500 meters. After a long freefall, I pulled the ripcord. It took five minutes to float down under the life-saving canopy before I landed on the southern shore of the Ammersee. My wounds required a stay in hospital and then I was sent on convalescent leave for several weeks. This was my 23rd sortie, my 16th and 17th victories.

With the Wehrmacht in headlong retreat in France, the largest number of Luftwaffe fighter sorties on the Normandy front was recorded on August 20 with 580 Focke-Wulf 190 As and Messerschmitt Bf 109 Gustavs present. Fighting against odds of 10 to 1, German fighter pilots paid a heavy price in blood for their interventions—more than a thousand of them were shot down over the course of many hundreds of air battles against USAAF Mustangs and Thunderbolts, and RAF Typhoons and Spitfires. In return for these terrible losses, these same German pilots carried out their duties to the limits of physical and mental endurance—more than 1,200 kill claims were filed between June 6 and August 31.

Hptm. Klaus Mietusch joined 7./JG 26 in September 1939 and two years later was Staffelkapitän. On July 5, 1943 he was appointed Kommandeur III./JG 26. His victory over a USAAF B-17 on July 25, 1943 was the first of 16 *Viermots* he was to claim. His 50th victory was a B-17 shot down over Cambrai on October 20, 1943. He was awarded the Knight's Cross after 63 victories, on March 26, 1944, but was killed in action on September 17, 1944.

On the afternoon of August 25, 1944, the Kommandeur of I./JG 4, Maj. Walter Hoeckner, taxiied out at Ziegenhain to lead his Gruppe on a transfer to France and the Western Front. Ogfr. Horst Jaekel, 3./JG 4 recalled:

> It was on August 25 that I saw Hoeckner kill himself at Ziegenhain. His fighter powered off but flipped over at a height of around 20 meters and smashed into the ground. Those pilots that were already airborne and those just lifting off were completely stunned … I almost met the same fate. The cockpits of our Me 109s were extremely cramped. With parachute, equipment, and personal items, it was sometimes difficult to get much leverage on the stick, wedged as it was in between our knees. On one takeoff my machine veered off to starboard without me being able to do much about it—my knees got in the way of the stick movement. Fortunately, I was already over the valley that ran along one side of the airfield. I was able to push the stick forward and pick up speed and managed to keep the aircraft under control by the skin of my teeth.

Aged nearly 30, Walter Hoeckner had been flying the Bf 109 since 1940. On June 25, 1941, as Staffelkapitän of 6./JG 77, he had claimed no fewer than eight SB-2s during a free-hunt sweep. At the time of his death he was a 68-victory Knight's Cross bearer, with 16 kills notched up in the West, of which at least six were four-engined bombers. The Bf 109 was a particularly unforgiving aircraft, both for the novice and the seasoned ace. The tendency of the Bf 109 to swing badly on landing and takeoff could of course be countered—but it required plenty of rudder. Redesigned and enlarged tail surfaces (with better aerodynamic profiling), Flettner rudder tabs controllable from the cockpit, the introduction of a taller tail wheel strut and larger main wheels giving better ground control and visibility were introduced, particularly on the high-powered AS variants to improve directional stability and reduce stick forces at high speed.

In early September JG 26 lost two of its *Experten*: on September 3, Lt. Karl Kempf (65 victories) was shot down and killed at the controls of Fw 190 A-8 Black 9, caught by 55th FG P-51s while taking off with 2. Staffel from Grimbergen. That same day the Kommandeur II./JG 26, the famous Hptm. "Bully" Lang (173 victories, including 29 in the West), was lost in action near St. Trond. On September 17, the Gruppenkommandeur III./JG 26, Hptm. Klaus Mietusch, was shot down

Fighter ace Walter Nowotny inspects a *Höhenjäger* test bed, a prototype for the superlative high-altitude interceptor, the Ta 152, that did not enter service until March 1945 with JG 301. The Fw 190 V32 GH+KV was designed as a DB 603 S-1-powered, high-altitude fighter, one of Kurt Tank's many projects powered by the big 445-liter DB 603 engine. Note the four-bladed propeller and pressurized cockpit.

over Arnhem by P-51s. Having led III./JG 26 with efficiency and courage in Normandy, he would be awarded the Oak Leaves posthumously for his 76 *Abschüsse* (including 16 bombers).

At that time, German factories were beginning series production of a revolutionary new aircraft: the Me 262 jet fighter. But it was still suffering from teething issues and could only be deployed in small numbers. At the same time the first production examples of the "long-nosed Dora," the Fw 190 D-9, were starting to come off the assembly lines at the Focke-Wulf plants at Cottbus and Sorau, and at Fiesler, Kassel-Waldau. Production amounted to four aircraft per day. By December and in the teeth of concerted bombing raids, production at the Marienburg plant in East Prussia peaked at eight Doras per day. Deliveries to service units began in early September 1944. The first Gruppe to convert to the Dora-9 was III/JG 54 under the leadership of the energetic and charismatic Kommandeur, Eastern Front ace Hptm. Robert Weiss. The pilots—many of whom were experienced ex-bomber aviators responding to Göring's appeal for volunteers for the defense of the Reich and untrained as fighters—initially viewed their new "hybrid" with unease, prompting a visit from the designer Kurt Tank, as Staffelkapitän Willi Heilmann reported:

> So this was Germany's greatest genius among aircraft designers and the pilots soon warmed to him. We learned that the Dora-9 was only an urgently needed interim solution chiefly because Junkers had in their yards large numbers of the Jumo 213 engine, originally built for the bomber force. His aim was the Ta 152, a high-altitude fighter with a ceiling of 42,000 feet, the best-engined aircraft in the world. It was practically ready for mass production.

The Dora could outclimb and outdive its BMW 801-powered predecessor with ease, and it possessed an excellent turning rate at speed. Kommandeur Weiss achieved the first victory on the type by shooting down a reconnaissance Spitfire of 541 Sqn on September 28, 1944. In early October two Staffeln of III. /JG 54, Oblt. Hans Dortenmann's 12. Staffel and Willi Heilmann's 9. Staffel, were assigned to fly top cover at Achmer for the Me 262s of the jet trials unit Kommando Nowotny. Tragedy struck on November 8. Helmut Rathjie of 12./JG 54 recalled:

> On this day 12. Staffel not only flew airfield cover but both 9. and 12. Staffeln were sent after fighter bombers. In the sky all hell was loose. My aircraft refused to start; therefore I was able to follow everything on the radio. There was a period of wild confusion. I heard Nowotny's voice, "Shit, my engine is on fire ..." It was his last flight.

The Kommandeur's Me 262, chased into low cloud by a 20th FG P-51, dived steeply into the ground exploding just prior to impact. The Austrian died with a score of 258 victories and a reputation that would elevate him to Tagjagd legend.

By November 1944, after 80 deliveries to III./JG 54, several other Jagdgruppen started to receive the new fighter, with II./JG 26 and III./JG 2 officially converting onto the Dora. Some machines also reached the Stab./JG 4 and II./JG 301. Nearly 200 D-9s had been produced by the end of 1944. Yet under the Allied aerial onslaught losses were heavy. III./JG 54 experienced a black day on December 29, 1944 losing over 20 machines including the Kommandeur, while losses on January 14, 1945—which saw a major USAAF raid on Berlin—amounted to a third of all Doras then in service.

Defense of the Reich

The months of September, October, and November 1944 saw some of the hardest fighting for the Luftwaffe aces. On September 11, 1944, I./JG 300, flying top cover, lost 13 Bf 109s without claiming a single victory. II.(Sturm)/JG 300 lost 13 Fw 190s to P-51 Mustangs, with ten pilots killed and two wounded, including Konrad Bauer, one of the most effective Focke-Wulf 190 pilots of II./JG 300 during the summer of 1944.

His wingman, Lt. Hans-Dieter Oehm, described him:

> Konrad Bauer was one of the best marksmen in the Gruppe. To the younger pilots he was the archetypal fighter pilot. Above all he drank far more than was good for him, both before and after sorties … which did not seem to affect his abilities as a pilot! At the time I was rather lacking in maturity and could be counted among his admirers. He had come from Jagdgeschwader 51 Mölders and had brought down a considerable number of Soviet aircraft in a short space of time. He seemed just as sure of himself against the Americans.

When Bauer was transferred in early 1944 to 2./JG 3 "Udet" operating on RVT duties, he had claimed a total of 18 VVS aircraft shot down on the Eastern Front. In the home defense, Bauer recorded his first victory over a bomber on April 18, when he shot down a USAAF B-17. He shot down another two on May 24. Bauer was shot down in Red 21 on September 11 in combat with P-51s (he claimed three of them). He made a successful belly-landing but was wounded after being strafed by P-51s while trapped in his cockpit—losing two fingers from his right hand. His injuries put him out of action until early 1945. He was awarded the Knight's Cross on October 31, 1944 for 34 victories, including 14 four-engined bombers and was recommended for the Oak Leaves but never received the award. "Pitt" Bauer flew 416 combat missions, his final tally around 57 enemy aircraft.

Konrad Bauer, 5./JG 300, seated on his Fw 190 Red 3: the inscription "Kornjark" is a reference to his favorite alcoholic drink.

Another view of Red 3 undergoing weapons synchronization. Bauer is at right.

On September 27, II./JG 300 assembled in a massed *Gefechtsverband* battle formation with II./JG 4 and IV./JG 3—some 120 *Sturm* aircraft escorted by Bf 109 fighters of I./JG 300—and struck at the 445th BG near Kassel. The scenes of death and destruction can barely be imagined as some 30 bombers went down—a record loss for the U.S. bombing offensive. Uffz. Ernst Schröder of 5./JG 300 described what he saw:

> It wasn't long before we came across a large group of B-24 Liberators. At our altitude they looked like a swarm of mosquitos, flying right in front of us, heading in the same direction. The silhouettes quickly grew larger because of our high speed. Suddenly, several of these big ships began to burn and to plunge down trailing fire and smoke—a *Sturm* unit flying ahead of us had begun the attack. Immediately, the sky was full of parachutes and wreckage, and we were flying right into it. That day I was testing a new Revi sight and I was able to open up at a much greater range than was normally the case—even before I had covered the remaining distance to my bomber, it was already in flames as a result of my six guns. Both port engines were burning. Then the huge bomber turned on its side and plunged. By now the neighboring machine was already smoking—I had only needed to slide-slip to open up again. Bright flames erupted from this machine. At high speed I tore past my victim, staring at the meter-long flames that were pouring out of the Liberator all the way back beyond the elevator. Then this great machine clumsily laid itself over on its back and went down.

Konrad Bauer standing on the wing of Red 1, flown by the Staka of 5./JG 300, Klaus Bretschneider.

In Profile:
Oblt. Hans-Martin Markhoff

Oblt. Hans-Martin Markhoff was Staffelkapitän of 8.(Sturm)/JG 4 in September 1944 and participated in the attack on the B-24s of the 445th BG over Kassel on September 27, 1944—one of the most serious reverses suffered by the Eighth Air Force during their bombing campaign over Germany:

> By mid-1944 I was an experienced fighter pilot, having flown many sorties on the Russian Front as wingman to one of JG 52's greatest aces, Hptm. Günther Rall. I had experienced the arduous conditions in the East—the constant moving from field to field—Kuban, Belgorod, Orel, Kharkov, the Ukraine, and the Crimea—temporary encirclements, sickness. Charged with screening the Kommandeur of III./JG 52, my chances of achieving victories in aerial combat were very limited—I hadn't been able to open my account at all.

An Fw 190 *Sturmbock* bores in on a B-24 Liberator from the rear. Hunkered down in his cockpit the pilot opens fire from close range, aiming for the wing fuel tanks and inboard engine ... strikes from the 3-cm cannon flare ...

Fw 190 A-8/R2 of II.(Sturm)/JG 4 during the fall of 1944.

Then in 1944 Rall himself was posted back to the Reichsverteidigung. Having witnessed a terrible air raid on Berlin while on leave in late 1943, I decided that my duty as a fighter pilot lay in defending my fellow citizens back home in Germany. So I volunteered to be a *Sturm* pilot. I wasn't afraid of ramming enemy bombers—I doubted whether such actions would ever be necessary if I got in close enough to use my armament.

On September 27, 1944 over Eisenach we closed on the four-engined bombers with total disregard to the stiff defensive fire they were putting up. Tracer was flying around our ears but there was only one thought in my mind—shooting down a bomber. The bombers' defensive ring of fire was broken through recklessly. Only after the four engines filled the target circle of the sight did we open fire. When we made our final attack, we approached from slightly above, then dove and opened fire … A miss of the giant monster was almost impossible at this distance. I could clearly recognize the faces of the gunners in their firing positions.

The 3-cm cannon were remarkably effective and wrought terrible destruction. Everything happened so quickly, my shells pumped into the bomber's wing-root and I could see a bright sheet of flame as it leaped from the huge fuselage. Pieces of debris whirled around me in the slipstream. Part of the bomber's tailfin came away. I took evasive action and dove under the huge machine.

Emerging from the bomber stream, we attempted to reform for a second pass but today, as more often than not, this was impossible … we could hear the cries in the headsets alerting us to the presence of enemy fighters … it was then every man for himself as we attempted to reach an aerodrome and put down. That day as I came in to Salzwedel I realized that I'd got problems with my landing gear and elected to put the machine down on its belly. Those machines from my Gruppe that had landed ahead of me were almost all displaying signs of damage. More than half our Fw 190s were missing … 7. Staffel was particularly hard hit. Having already been reinforced with 6. and 8. Staffel pilots, the Staffel now lost its Kapitän, Oblt. Zehart, who was reported missing near Braunschweig.

After the war Markhoff trained as an architect but never told his family of his war record. It wasn't until the late 1970s, just a few years before his death, that he told his teenage son about his career in the Jagdwaffe. Like his son, Markhoff himself wore his hair long and was a big fan of the Rolling Stones. He added a poignant footnote to his description of combat:

If you publish these accounts please convey to the reader that such events must never again be allowed to take place. I'm not proud of my successes and what I did during the war. We all of us merely reacted to the pressures of those times. Today I wish that they had never occurred.

Oblt Hans-Martin Markhoff was Staffelkapitän of 8./JG 4 in September 1944.

Ernst Schröder's Fw 190 A-8 Red 19. Although he flew in the Sturmgruppe, Schröder had claimed a number of P-51s during the summer of 1944 and flew an unarmored machine as top cover for the 5./JG 300 *Sturmböcke*. Note his victory stick on the foot step. A rare II.Gruppe bar is just visible on the rear fuselage.

During November 1944 the day fighter pilots suffered tremendous losses—some 244 pilots killed on operations for barely 150 Allied machines downed. Meanwhile the Wehrmacht had been preparing in the greatest secrecy a counter-offensive codenamed *Frühlingswind* and later referred to as the "Battle of the Bulge." This time, with strict radio silence, the attack was not compromised by Ultra. The offensive caught the Allied armies in the West by surprise and the Luftwaffe was able to inflict high losses on medium bomber formations forced to operate unescorted; no fewer than 30 B-26 Marauders were credited to IV./JG 3 on December 23.

However, the *Jagdflieger* would suffer severe losses in the face of Allied numerical superiority once the opponent regrouped. On December 24, JG 77 was caught up with P-47s and Spitfires over the Ardennes. Kommodore Maj. Johannes Wiese was bounced by a group

Kommodore JG 300 Walther Dahl in the cockpit of his Blue 13 displaying the "B-17 in the gunsight" emblem. According to his own account, Dahl was flown to Hitler's HQ at Rastenburg on September 15, 1944 to explain his unit's heavy losses on September 11, 12 and their "black day" of September 13. Barely a month later Dahl was dismissed from his command after refusing to order the inexperienced pilots of III./JG 300 to counter an American bombing raid in poor weather conditions. Dahl was nonetheless appointed Inspector of Day Fighters in January 1945 and, according to his memoir, continued to fly combat sorties, returning his 100th victory on March 1, 1945.

Pilots of 14.(Sturm)/JG 3, alongside Uffz. Oskar Bösch's Fw 190 A-8/R2 Black 14, accounted for six of the 30 Marauders shot down by IV. Gruppe on December 23. Bösch is second right; first right is Uffz. Helmut Keune. Of the 13 pilots pictured here, no fewer than ten were killed or reported missing in action, an indication of the odds faced by the day fighter pilots in late 1944.

of Spitfires, his wingman downed on their first pass. His Bf 109 G-10 was also cornered and badly shot up. Wiese bailed out at 9,000 meters; when he finally pulled the cord, he realized to his horror that the ground rushing to him was only 80 meters away. The brutal landing caused him some serious injuries and he spent much of the winter in hospital. Hptm. Lothar Baumann, Kommandeur of I./JG 77, was less fortunate: he crashed to his death in his Bf 109 G-14. Oblt. Iring Englisch, Staffelkapitän of 4./JG 77, was also killed that day, with nine victories to his credit. In total, nine Bf 109 G-14s of I./JG 77 failed to return on December 24, 1944. Erich Leie was preferred to Siegfried Freytag as Wiese's replacement, while Freytag would subsequently go on to convert onto the Me 262.

At that time, there was immemse fatigue in the ranks of the veterans. The Kommodore of JG 1, Herbert Ihlefeld, was no longer flying much by late 1944. And on December 27, 1944, the Kommandeur I./JG 1, Major Hans Ehlers, led 18 Fw 190s over the Ardennes front at low altitude on a strafing sortie in support of the German ground offensive. He was heard ordering his pilots to stay in close formation even as Mustangs dove down on them. Ignoring the radio warnings from his wingmen, he was then shot down for the 13th time—and killed. Only three I./JG 1 Fw 190s returned. Ehlers had led the Gruppe since April 1944 and had been awarded the Knight's Cross in June 1944. He had accumulated at least 52 victories—including 23 *Viermots*—and was apparently at the end of his rope. This case can be compared to that of Oblt. Peter Reischer. On December 18, this Austrian officer was leading III./JG 26 but carefully avoiding combat. Reprimanded by his superiors, this 19-victory ace was forced to fly a second sortie but could not bring himself to enter enemy airspace. He then put down again at Plantlünne, rolled to the end of the runway, turned off the engine of his 190, and shot himself in the head.

In Profile:
Huppertz, Schenk, and Hartmann

Fw 190 A-8, Hptm. Hubert Huppertz, Kommandeur III./JG 2, June 6, 1944. Huppertz claimed his first victory, a Spitfire, over Dunkirk on May 28, 1940 with 6./JG 51. His tally at the start of June 1944 was around 70 confirmed kills. He claimed five Allied fighters downed on June 6, 1944, but was shot down and killed in the vicinity of Caen two days later, on June 8.

Bf 109 G-10 Red 5, 2./JG 300, "Timo-Schenko" flown by Wilhelm-Friedrich Schenk. Schenk was Staffelführer of 2./JG 300 as the unit was deployed on the Oder Front in February 1945, strafing the advanced Soviet columns approaching Berlin. His machine displayed the inscription "Timo-Schenko," a play on words of his name and that of the Red Army commander leading the assault on Berlin during the *Endkampf*, the final battle.

Bf 109 G-6, Erich Hartmann Kommandeur I./JG 53, Veszprem, Hungary, February 1945. Often thought to be a G-14, Hartmann's own logbook confirms this machine to have been a G-6. The upper-surface white winter camo finish features a curious "spider's web" overspray. Note the missing DF loop and the absence of an antenna mast.

On December 23, over Bonn, Obfw. Heinrich Bartels (15./JG 27) was reported missing. He had been credited with 99 victories and had been awarded the Knight's Cross at the end of 1942. During the Normandy fighting, he had downed 11 Allied fighters. His body was not found until 1968, near Bad Godesberg.

On July 15, 1944, Maj. Ehlers (middle, wearing his Knight's Cross) celebrated his 30th birthday at Cuissai in the midst of the battle for Normandy. On December 27, he was shot down by Mustangs and killed, along with 15 of the I./JG 1 Fw 190s he was leading on a strafing sortie over the Ardennes.

Crash landing of Bf 109 G-14 (W.Nr. 462818) flown by Fw. Henning of the Gruppenstab of III./JG 3 during a transfer flight from Erfurt-Bindersleben in December 1944. The aircraft is sporting the white fuselage *Rumpfband* assigned to JG 3 for the defense of the Reich.

Bf 109 G-6s of II./JG 5 in the snow of the Far North, February 1944. Black 4, assigned to Oblt. Theo Weissenberger, is seen here taxiing out to the runway alongside Kommandeur Hptm. Horst Carganico's "Mickey Mouse." Carganico was subsequently appointed Kommandeur I./JG 5 before being killed in a landing accident in May 1944.

The East, 1944

Victory records in the East in 1944 increasingly list only JG 51, 52, and 54—in addition to *Abschüsse* returned by JG 5 and an increasing number of ground support or armed reconnaissance units. In a change of tactics, a number of Gruppen (JG 3, I. and II./JG 5, and III./JG 54) had been recalled to the Reich to defend *Festung Deutschland*—Fortress Germany—while a large number of ground support units (SG 2 and 10) equipped with Fw 190s replaced the fighters.

On January 23, 1944, Hptm. Gerhard Barkhorn, Gruppenkommandeur II./JG 52, returned from his 1,000th combat sortie. In total he flew 1,104 *Feindflüge*, some 500 of which involved low-level attacks on ground targets.

Kriegstagebuch (War Diary) extract, JG 52

Tuesday, January 18, 1944

Uffz. Alois Seibel, 3. Staffel, killed. When downing a Boston 5 km west of Darjewo his Bf 109 took hits. About 10 minutes later, on the return flight, his machine suddenly exploded.

Fhj. Fw. Otto Fönnekold, 5. Staffel, achieved his 100th victory.

Sunday, 23 January 1944

Hptm. Gerhard Barkhorn, Kommandeur II. Gruppe, returned from his 1,000th *Feindflug*. He is the first fighter pilot in the world to achieve this high number of combat sorties. Lt. Erich Hartmann returned his 175th air victory, an La-7, at 13.27. Fhj. Fw. Heinz Sachsenberg, 6. Staffel, shot down an Airacobra at 07.25. His 60th victory.

Tuesday, January 25, 1944

Lt. Helmut Lipfert, leader of 6. Staffel shot down a Yak-1 at 12.27 and a Boston at 12.40 for his 87th and 88th victories.

Thursday, January 27, 1944

Lt. Franz Schall, 3. Staffel, flew a free hunt with his Rottenflieger, Uffz. Anton Resch, in the Kertsch area. Over Kertsch, *Luftkampf* [dogfight] with 6 Airacobras, during which Uffz. Resch was wounded. In a battle over Kolonka, at about 06.45, Uffz. Ludwig Vogel of 5. Staffel was slightly wounded.

Friday, 28 January 1944

Award of the German Cross in Gold:

Oblt. Wilhelm Batz, Adju. II. Gruppe;

Lt. Helmut Lipfert, Führer 6. Staffel;

Ofw. Walter Janke, 2. Staffel pilot.

On January 22, 1944, near Berditschew, Uffz. Otto Gaiser of 10./JG 51 was reported missing after a fierce battle. Having arrived in late 1942 in the unit, he had 68 *Abschüsse* to his credit and received the Knight's Cross after his death. On February 5, 1944, Fw. Hans Waldmann of 6./JG 52 (temporarily detached as *Jagdlehrer*—instructor—to Erg. Gruppe Ost) received the Knight's Cross for his 85 *Luftsiege*. Promoted to Kapitän of 4./JG 52, he accumulated 40 more victories over Soviet aircraft before fighting in June 1944 in Normandy. In three sorties on February 26, Lt. Erich Hartmann (9./JG 52) claimed ten victories, including five in an 18-minute period and his 200th that afternoon. On March 2, he was awarded the Oak Leaves for 202 victories, including some 24 returned over the previous two months.

On February 23, Uffz. Otto Würfel of 9./JG 51 hit his wingman near Rogatschew. Captured, he died in December in a Soviet PoW camp. He also joined the unit in 1942, had 79 victories to his credit and was awarded the Knight's Cross in May 1944. Two days later, one of the leading day fighters of the Tagjagd perished. Maj. Siegfried Schnell, a Luftwaffe veteran since 1936 and one of the top scorers in the West, was Kommandeur IV./JG 54. He had added three victories over Soviet machines to his 90 in the West when he was killed in action south of Narwa. "Wumm" Schnell was an Oak Leaves bearer.

Otto Gaiser, an ace of 10./JG 51, seen here at Smolensk in 1943. He returned his first victory on March 16, 1943, north of Wjasma and by late summer 1943, he had 35 victories. On September 26, 1943 he claimed five Yak-1s and a further three Soviet machines the following day. On January 15, 1944 he downed two Yak-4 fighters and two IL-2s to reach 66 victories. Airborne on January 22 in Bf 109 G-6 White 11 (W.Nr. 140229), he was caught up in combat with four IL-2s and failed to return. It was assumed that he had made a forced landing behind enemy lines.

Lt. Hans Dammers of 9./JG 52 receiving the Knight's Cross from his Staka, Hermann Graf.

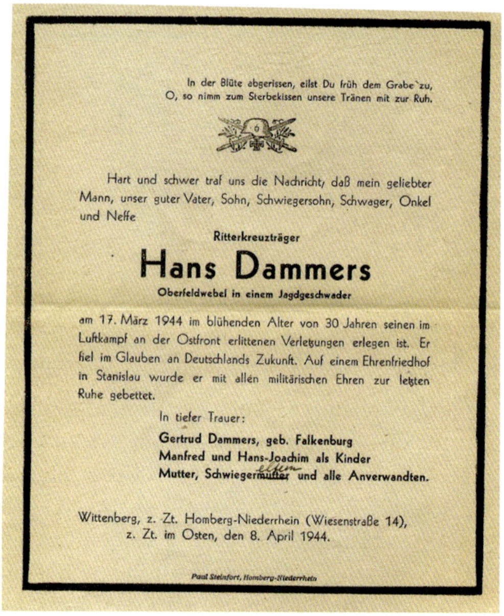

In der Blüte abgerissen, eilst Du früh dem Grabe zu,
O, so nimm zum Sterbekissen unsere Tränen mit zur Ruh.

Hart und schwer traf uns die Nachricht, daß mein geliebter Mann, unser guter Vater, Sohn, Schwiegersohn, Schwager, Onkel und Neffe

Ritterkreuzträger

Hans Dammers

Oberfeldwebel in einem Jagdgeschwader

am 17. März 1944 im blühenden Alter von 30 Jahren seinen im Luftkampf an der Ostfront erlittenen Verletzungen erlegen ist. Er fiel im Glauben an Deutschlands Zukunft. Auf einem Ehrenfriedhof in Stanislau wurde er mit allen militärischen Ehren zur letzten Ruhe gebettet.

In tiefer Trauer:

Gertrud Dammers, geb. Falkenburg
Manfred und Hans-Joachim als Kinder
Mutter, Schwiegermutter und alle Anverwandten.

Wittenberg, z. Zt. Homberg-Niederrhein (Wiesenstraße 14),
z. Zt. im Osten, den 8. April 1944.

Paul Steinfort, Homberg-Niederrhein

Lt. Hans Dammers' death notice.

In April 1944, Hitler awarded Oak Leaves to (from left): Alfred Grislawski, Emil Lang, Günther Schack, Otto Kittel, and Anton Hafner. Grislawski wears a Romanian pilot badge while his four comrades wear the German Cross in Gold. The award of this latter cross usually preceded the award of the Knight's Cross.

On March 13, Lt. Hans Dammers (9./JG 52) had to evacuate his Bf 109 G-6 Yellow 9 (W.Nr. 20162) at Oleschin, hit by the debris of an La-5 he was shooting down. He apparently opened his parachute too early; the canvas caught on a wing and the hapless pilot went down with his machine. He died four days later in hospital. Dammers had joined 7./JG 52 in the summer of 1941 and won the Knight's Cross for his 51 *Luftsiege*. At his death, he had 113 victories and a significant number of ground kills (locomotives, armored vehicles, etc).

On March 19, 1944, Lt. Walter Wolfrum, 5./JG 52, returned six *Abschüsse*, including three IL-2 Sturmoviks and a Boston, for victories 39–44, barely a week later downing another four VVS machines to advance his score to 51 victories. In the hands of an experienced pilot, the Bf 109 was still the "ace-maker" of the early war years but was at the point of being outclassed by newer Soviet fighters, such as the Yak-3 which was about to enter service.

During the summer of 1944 the Third Reich endured huge reverses on both the Eastern and Western fronts. After barely eight weeks of bitter fighting, the Normandy front had collapsed with the Allies closing the Falaise Pocket. Furthermore, the Eastern Front was

JG 54 pilots pose with the Geschwader green heart emblem. From left: Raumpach, Hans-Joachim Kroschinski, Karl Brill, and Fritz Luck. Obfw. Kroschinski was seriously wounded (loss of sight and one foot) in combat on December 21, 1944 over Courland where I. and II./JG 54 faced overwhelming odds. He was awarded the Knight's Cross for his 76 victories.

Staffelkapitän 1./JG 52 Lt. Walter Wolfrum—fighter ace and post-war West German aerobatics champion.

seriously and rapidly contracting. The Soviets launched their first major summer offensive—codenamed *Bagration*—shortly after D-Day and threatened the total annihilation of Army Group Center. Hitler believed the blow would fall farther south. Ritter von Greim's Luftflotte 6, covering Ernst Busch's central sector, had available only 100 ground-attack aircraft and 100 fighters, the bulk of his forces being outmoded bomber types. The offensive was launched on June 22, the skies above Army Group Center thick with wave after wave of VVS machines. During July Operation *Bagration* virtually annihilated the most formidable assemblage of German military might. In addition, there was the failed assassination attempt on Hitler on July 20. On August 29, Bucharest fell to the Soviets and Romania changed sides.

JG 52 ace Erich Hartmann's exploits through the summer of 1944 were a counter to the constant barrage of bad news from the fronts. Hartmann had passed 250 victories in June over Romania and was fast approaching 300; with a Propaganda Kompanie (PK) unit at the scene Hartmann filed 19 claims in two days—August 23 and 24. On August 24, Hartmann claimed his victories 299–303 over the Soviet beachhead of Sandomierz across the Vistula—all four were P-39s. According to Russian research the only unit equipped with Aircobras providing cover to Sandomierz were from the elite 9th Guards Fighter Aviation Division (GIAD) led by Polkovnik (Col.) Aleksandr Pokryshkin—they sustained no losses in air combat that day. One Soviet P-39 pilot was reported missing after becoming separated from his comrades.

On the German side cameramen and PK reporters were ever-present to record the exploits, not just of Hartmann, but of all the aces of JG 52. Oblt. Rudolf Trenkel, Staffelkapitän of 2./ JG 52 returned his 100th on July 14, 1944, while July saw Hartmann's former wingman and his successor as Staffelkapitän, Fhj. Fw Hans-Joachim Birkner (9./JG 52), progress his victory tally to eighty-eight.

At the controls of his Bf 109G-6 (W.Nr. 163631) White 6, leading ace and now Staffelkapitän 1./JG 52 Walter Wolfrum returned ten victories on July 16 before being seriously wounded, shot down by Airacobras of the 9th Fighter Aviation Regiment (IAP):

> the Soviet offensive mounted from the area of Tarnopol towards Lvov hit us head on with all its might. I./JG 52 was the only fighter formation for far and wide. On the first day I returned four victories but by that evening, of the 14 machines in my 1. Staffel, four had sustained combat damage and were no longer serviceable. There was no way of replacing them. On the following day we flew without respite. I had flown two sorties before 09:00. During my first two sorties I engaged strong formations of IL-2s, covered by Yak-9 and Airacobra fighters. Each time I managed to down two Yaks. During my third sortie, I shot down four aircraft

> out of formation of 12 La-5s within a space of a few minutes. Eight victories in three sorties had had no effect whatsoever. By midday the sound of artillery fire approaching our field could be heard and it was time to evacuate. Around 15:00 I taxied out with our last four serviceable machines and soon after getting airborne an incoming Soviet bombing raid was reported over the radio—it was difficult to miss them. Around 100 Pe-2 and Mitchell bombers, covered by a similar number of fighters—the biggest enemy formation I had ever seen up to that point—were heading for Lemberg. I made several attempts to get through to the bombers and in the confusion, I shot down a Yak-9, but broke off as my wingman had been hit and was turning for home. I escorted him back over friendly territory. Now I was on my own. In the meantime, I noticed around a dozen P-39 Airacobras flying top cover for the whole formation. I had a chance to do something with these types. I pulled away, gained altitude up to 9,000 meters, and then went after the Airacobras. In the ensuing dogfight I nailed one, registering three, four, five hits. At the same time, I had become the hunted. I spotted another P-39 lining up dangerously close behind me, almost in a firing position. I loosed off one more burst to finish off the Airacobra in front of me before I could pull the emergency brake—throwing my aircraft into a spin to spoil the aim of the fighter behind me.
>
> As I threw the machine into a tight curve, pulling the stick back into my stomach, my machine flipped over onto its back, I felt a light blow in my right hip, which instantly made me feel nauseous. I fell into a bank of cumulus cloud below me. After a few spins—four turns, five turns, six, seven—I chopped the throttle, threw the stick forward and dove away. As I pulled up, I momentarily blacked out due to G forces and as the gray veil lifted, I pulled up steeply, right into the pack of Airacobras. I was immediately set upon by the enemy fighters but dove back into the nearest cloud, repeating the maneuver until I finally lost the pursuers.

Badly injured in his hip but incredibly lucky, Lt. Wolfrum managed to return to his forward landing strip at Peloniczna. As soon as he touched down, he passed out, while his aircraft rolled to a halt with the engine idling. Wolfrum was hospitalized for six months, in the meantime (on July 27) receiving the Knight's Cross for his 126 victories. After returning to the front in February 1945, he added nine more to his tally. During his combat service he was himself shot down 12 times and injured on four occasions.

Elsewhere, another Karaya Staffel pilot, 80-victory ace Lt. Herbert Bachnick, crashed to his death in East Prussia on August 7, 1944, his Yellow 4 (W.Nr. 166065) shot down by P-51s escorting B-17s airborne from the Ukranian field of Mirogod. He attempted an emergency landing but the aircraft hit a railway embankment near Myslowitz. Bachnick was officially credited with 80 enemy machines in

Staffelkapitän Fhj. Fw. Hans-Joachim Birkner (9./JG 52).

373 combat missions. His tally included 41 IL-2 Sturmoviks. Bachnick had joined JG 52 in December 1942. He won his first three aerial victories on July 5, 1943 over Kursk. From there his tally increased rapidly and by late 1943 he had already returned 47 *Abschüsse*. In March 1944 he recorded 27 Russian aircraft downed, including four on March 12 (59–62), five on March 15 (63–67), and five more on March 19 (72–76). He was awarded the Knight's Cross on July 27 after 79 victories. On July 24 Lublin fell and three days later Lemberg (Lwow—eastern Poland) was captured.

Lt. Anton Resch of 3./JG 52 returned seven victories on August 26, 1944 to take his score to 44. Elsewhere Lt. Franz Schall of 3./JG 52 claimed his 100th on August 31, 1944 in his Yellow 13, having shot down 11 on August 26 (victories 83–93) and returned no fewer than 13 on August 31. These exploits saw him posted back to Germany to the Me 262 operational test unit, Erprobungskommando Nowotny.

On August 31, with Romania now out of the war, JG 52 fell back to Hungary. Landing at Budak, 136-victory *Experte* Oblt. Otto Fönnekold (5. Staffel) was killed by a ground-strafing 52nd FG P-51. The landmark 10,000th victory for the Geschwader was returned by the Kommandeur I./JG 52, Alfred Borchers, on September 2, 1944, his 118th kill.

During the five-month period from April to August 1944 Romania was caught in the crossfire from all sides. Although dependent on the Eastern Front, the country came under heavy attack from American bombers. Benefiting from good bases around Foggia, Italy, the USAAF launched some 20 large-scale raids targeting Romanian refineries and fuel transport facilities. Most of them were round trips, but American command introduced shuttle missions, their aircraft departing Foggia and landing in the USSR before returning to Italy two or three days later. This tactic allowed more precise attacks but was still held in suspicion by the Soviets who were reluctant to help their American ally. There were therefore only a handful of such shuttles actually flown. But, during these raids, local defenses faced P-51 and P-38 escorts enjoying numerical superiority.

III./JG 77 found itself directly in the firing line under Kommandeur, Hptm. Emil Omert. However, Omert was shot down and killed while hanging from his parachute on April 24—he had returned around 70 victories in 700 combat flights.

Oblt. Otto Fönnekold, long-time Staffelkapitän of 5./JG 52, was killed on August 31, 1944. According to Obermaier, he shot down three 52nd FG P-51s on his last sortie, flying Bf 109 G-6 Black 9, but there is little evidence for this.

On May 5, at least 485 U.S. bombers returned to Ploesti with an escort of 285 fighters. Thanks to Ultra, the Allies knew that only about 50 German fighters defended the oil infrastructure. The indigenous Romanian IAR fighters along with the complement of Bf 109s flown by the Romanian Air Force barely counted. On the other hand, the Flak dispersed around the objectives remained dangerous. In some bitter fighting III./JG 77 claimed nine B-24s (plus two HSS), one P-51, and one P-47. Nineteen B-17/B-24s were lost that day, as were one P-47, and two P-38s. Uffz. Karl-Heinz Böttner claimed the P-51 (his 12th victory and first over a fighter) but his Gustav took hits in the engine. He had to carry out an emergency landing shortly afterward, gear up in a field near Mizil (damage to the aircraft assessed at 10 percent). The pilot was unharmed.

On May 7, over 400 bombers attempted to strike a fatal blow at railway infrastructure in and around Bucharest. III./JG 77 does not seem to have been able to get close to the bombers that were well protected by 200 P-38 and P-51 fighters. Three Lightnings were claimed (only one was in fact lost) but the German pilots fought for their lives. Böttner remembered that this was his hardest fight so far: "I was chased for a long time by four P-51s who riddled me with bullets. However, I was able to put down again safely at Mizil where I found my comrade Hackler who had had a similar experience."

On June 24, II. and III. Gruppen of JG 52 took on Fifteenth Air Force Liberators as they headed for the Romanian refineries. Staka 6./JG 52 Oblt. Helmut Lipfert recalled how startled he was upon seeing 300 four-engined bombers flying in formation—his Staffel consisted of only nine Bf 109 Gs. They claimed two B-24s, credited to Lipfert himself and his wingman, Uffz. Tammen. Nevertheless, their mission was little short of a disaster:

> Tammen and I landed at Buzeat. We clambered out of our machines and congratulated each other on our successes, as well as the fact that we were still alive. We were again walking our dear solid ground, but unfortunately the two of

III./JG 77 Kommandeur Hptm. Emil Omert (center with Knight's Cross) with a visiting theatrical troupe alongside his Bf 109 Gustav at Mizil, early 1944. His Kommandeur chevrons are just visible. To the left of the Kommandeur is the Staffelkapitän 8./JG 77, Oblt. Erhardt Niese.

On January 22, 1944, to underline the importance of defending Romania's refineries, the Inspector of Fighters Galland visited III./JG 77 at Mizil.

To combat U.S. bombers over Romania, III./JG 77 had a Staffel of Bf 109 G-6s toting air-to-air rocket launchers. Seen with pipe (second right) is young Sudeten Uffz. Anton Hackl. Arriving at 8./JG 77 at the end of 1943, "Tonschi" Hackl claimed a B-24 over Ploesti on April 4, 1944, but was shot down and killed the next day in his Black 8 during the course of another raid on Ploesti.

A flaming B-17 falls over Cimpina, Romania.

A Knight's Cross bearer seen examining the wreck of a downed P-38 somewhere in Romania. The U.S. twin-boom fighter had been on a shuttle mission from Italy to the Soviet Union. The ace is possibly Oblt. Wilhelm Batz (5./JG 52) who ended the war with 257 victories and the Oak Leaves.

In September 1944, at Riga, Kapitän Kittel won the 1,000th victory credited to his 2./JG 54.

Two Oak Leaves winners from JG 54 seen during summer 1944 in the East: Hptm. Horst Ademeit, Kommandeur I./JG 54 (left) and Kommandeur II./JG 54 Maj. Erich Rudorffer.

Hptm. Horst Ademeit, Kommandeur I./JG 54, seen shortly after dismounting from his Fw 190 A-6 <<+ (W.Nr. 550528) during the summer of 1944.

> us were the only ones who got away unscathed. Five of our men were shot down. Two were killed on the spot, and the third was executed by Mustangs while he hung in his [parachute] harness. Lt. Ewald managed to get clear of his machine—enveloped in flames—at the very last moment, but he was so badly burnt that he had to leave us for quite some time. Another pilot parachuted to safety. Two other machines were riddled by return fire and had to make emergency landings—one of them at the first airfield that came in sight.

On August 23, during the takeover of Bucharest, the Red Army took captive some of III./JG 77's aces in hospitals, such as Ofw. Johann Pichler (1940 veteran, 52 victories), and Lt. Günther Schmitz (arrived in 1942, 36 victories). Pichler, who eventually returned from captivity, learned that he had been awarded the Knight's Cross four days before his capture.

In the far north, an often-neglected sector, the loss of Lt. Jakob Norz was a tough blow for JG 5. This Bavarian, born in 1920, had led a diverse career, having started the war as a night fighter in I./NJG 2. In early 1942, he became a day fighter and joined JG 51 before moving to 7./JG 5. On March 5, 1943, shot down over the tundra, he had managed to regain his lines after a long march. On March 26, 1944, as an Oberfeldwebel, he was awarded the Knight's Cross for his 74 *Luftsiege*. He would reach 117 when he died on September 16, 1944. Following an engine problem during combat, he tried to put down his Bf 109 but the machine flipped and he was killed.

Two JG 52 aces, Hartmann and Barkhorn, at Csor, Hungary, in October 1944. At the time, their combined tally was 580 victories. Barkhorn enjoyed an immense amount of luck during his wartime career. He died on January 8, 1983, two days after sustaining injuries in a car crash which killed his wife Christa.

Bavarian Jakob Norz, 7./JG 5, in the insipid sunshine of the far north.

After a number of years in the West, Lt. Eberhard Burath flew with III./JG 51 during the summer of 1944, having been posted to the East on June 6, while his former comrades were committed over Normandy. His diary notes for the summer of 1944 make for interesting reading:

> when I arrived at JG 51 Maj. Losigkeit was extremely pleased to see me again, given the long period of time that we had spent together in JG 1. However, when it came to flying the Bf 109, I was a raw beginner and had to make numerous training flights, before going to Hptm. Schack's 9. Staffel based in Kowel. The landscape under my wings—after so long flying over western Europe and Germany—was now foreign and hostile. We spent the days at cockpit readiness … long days from 02:00 to 23:00, sweating like dogs as we roasted in our machines. On June 26 the *Alarmrotte* was scrambled … against Mustangs! We later found out they were escorting bombers flying a shuttle raid that had landed at Poltawa.
>
> On August 15 we shifted to Tilsit … by now we were flying over the Reich—which gave us reason to reflect. With Hptm. Brendel's Gruppe we flew numerous sorties over the Baltic territories. On August 28 in a Rotte with Maj. Losigkeit we encountered Airacobras—the only enemy aircraft operating over 5,000-meter altitudes. The Major claimed one shot down. On September 23, III. Gruppe had a very successful day—we came upon a formation of [six] Bostons heading for the port of Libau and shot them all down. In the aftermath only a handful of the typical square-shaped Russian parachutes could be seen drifting to the ground.

During September, JG 51 recorded 104 victories, followed by 195 in October—this number including 97 Sturmoviks, and 29 Boston and Pe-2 medium bombers. Individual successes abounded. Kommandeur Brendel was credited with 16 victories during this period. One short of that number was Staffelkapitän 10./JG 5 Lt. Anton Hafner; one of the three IL-2 s he claimed on October 16 was his 200th. The following day he bagged a Pe-2 and a Yak-7 but in a low-level dogfight his Bf 109G-6 (W.Nr. 442013) Black 1 hit a tree and crashed. "Toni" Hafner, JG 51's most successful pilot with 204 victories, was killed instantly. JG 51 continued to fight during 1945 along the Baltic coast and over East Prussia against overwhelming Soviet superiority.

Siegfried Lemke, 1./JG 2 ace, was promoted Leutnant after his successes in Italy. By the time of the D-Day landings, he was Staffelführer in 1./JG 2, claiming three victories on June 7, 1944. He was awarded the Knight's Cross on June 11, for 44 victories.

The Mediterranean, 1944

The British defeat in the Dodecanese—one of the last German victories of the war—had effectively reinforced Germany's presence in southeastern Europe. In addition, the Allies were mired in southern Italy. On January 22, the Allied Operation *Shingle* landing took place at Anzio/Nettuno with the aim of taking Rome. Kesselring's forces, reacting quickly, locked the invaders in the beachead for several weeks.

Heavily outnumbered, the local Tagjagd (JG 53 and 77) were briefly supported by II./JG 51 while I./JG 4 flew as replacements for III./JG 77. On February 20, I./JG 2 arrived in northern Italy. It had been operating over southern France, providing cover for Axis shipping. I./JG 2 was primarily equipped with the Fw 190—1., 2., and 3. Staffeln flew the Fw 190 A-6 and A-7—while 4./JG 2 flew the Bf 109 G-6. The Gruppe spent some five weeks in Italy and according to Geschwader records, claimed 52 victories, far more than other German units

Lemke alongside the rudder of his Fw 190 A-7 (W.Nr. 430674) marked with 48 kills.

A Bf 109 G-6 with wing-mounted cannon—the *Kanonenboot*. Based in northern Italy, these "gunboats" were used against *Viermots*.

operating over the battlefront in the same period. 1. Staffel filed at least 30 claims, most of these being credited to the ace Lt. Siegfried Lemke.

On March 3, 200 B-17s and 80 B-24s escorted by 50 P-47s bombed rail installations and hubs in and around Rome—I./JG 2 claimed five B-24s and four P-47s. Two were credited to Lemke, taking his tally to 23 victories. On March 19, Lemke was credited with downing three Spitfires, a feat that was the subject of a two-page account by a war correspondent. His third victim was shot down over the sea, but Lemke was also forced to ditch after his engine caught fire. He spent much of that day in his life-raft before managing to swim ashore. He subsequently rowed back out to sea to rescue one of the American pilots he had downed: 52nd FG pilot 2Lt. Robert Boyd.

Alongside the few units of the Repubblica Sociale Italiana (RSI) Air Force equipped with the Bf 109, the fighter Gruppen may have been active over the Anzio beachhead—usually supporting the Fw 190 *Jabos* of SG 4—but could do no more than delay the inevitable. On March 14 the ace and Staffelkapitän 3./JG 2 Hptm. Adalbert Sommer was shot down and killed. Sommer had spent most of the war with III./JG 52 in the East and had returned his 52nd victory on February 29, and his 53rd on March 3. On March 21, Uffz. Rudolf Wirtgen of 1./JG 2 became an ace after downing his fifth Spitfire in ten days.

Northern Italy was attacked from all sides, with the Allies having bases in Foggia and Corsica. Their bombers even crossed the Alps to attack Austria and Bavaria. In the south of the Reich, they encountered JG 27 protecting the Munich area. On March 26, Lt.

Oblt. Günther Seeger (JG 53) received the Knight's Cross in early 1944.

Oblt. Seeger (right, on the spinner) as Staffelkapitän 7./JG 53 in October 1944 operating in the defense of the Reich. His parents' house in Offenbach was destroyed in an Allied bombing raid in December 1943, killing his mother and severely injuring his father.

Kommandeur Jürgen Harder of I./ JG 53 seen alongside his *Kanonenboot* Chevron Triangle undergoing maintenance at Maniago, Italy, early 1944.

A fine portrait of Lt. Ernst-Wilhelm Reinert. The photo hints at the fact that his sunny personality—*Ich war immer ein sunny boy*—at times displeased his superiors.

Reinert describing a dogfight, somewhere in Italy. Appointed Staffelkapitän 3./JG 77 in September 1943, he fell ill in April 1944. When he returned to the front, it was as Staffelkapitän 1./JG 27 based in Austria. He moved to 12./JG 27 and led the Staffel against U.S. bombers raiding the Reich from Foggia. He was subsequently appointed Kommandeur IV./27, and deployed over Normandy where he returned three victories. Post-war he studied medicine and then served in the Bundesluftwaffe, the Western German Air Force.

During their advance up Italy, the Western allies captured aircraft like this Bf 109 G-6 of the "Ace of Spades."

Allied captures also included this II./JG 77 "gunboat."

Günther Seeger (a veteran of JG 2), attached to the Stab JG 53, finally received the Knight's Cross for his 46 victories, all won in the West. His last victory in Italy was claimed on January 29, a B-26 downed over the Tiber estuary. He was subsequently transferred to 4./JG 53 operating over the Reich before being appointed Staffelkapitän 7./JG 53 later in the year.

During these months of fierce fighting without much hope, I./JG 4 lost their Kommandeur. On 22 January, Hptm. Franz Hahn was shot down near Littorio. A fighter pilot since 1939, he had much experience in the West and had returned around 20 *Luftsiege*.

On February 3, Hptm. Herbert Puschmann (leading 6./JG 51) was killed near Civitavecchia in combat with a force of B-26 Marauders heading for Rome. Puschmann had arrived at the unit shortly before *Barbarossa*. At the time of his death, he had some 57 victories to his name, 43 of them in the East. The Knight's Cross was awarded posthumously. The impact on young pilots of the gradual loss of aces is well described by one of his pilots, Uffz. Alfons Schertl:

Hptm. "Puschi" Puschmann, Staffelkapitän 6./JG 51, during a break. Puschmann, much appreciated by his comrades, was killed in February 1944 near Civitavecchia.

Uffz. Heinz Girnth's Black 11 of III./JG 53 (8. Staffel) at Villa Orba. Girnth filed around 11 claims.

Herbert was our most skilled pilot; although taciturn, he formed the link between the old and the new generation of aviators. Cool and thoughtful, never nervous, always good-natured and ready to help, he was a comrade, a genuine one. With him, we spoke frankly with an open heart … He took care of the new boys, was our savior in air combat, our friend and our spiritual father, all in one. When we lost him the Gruppe lost its moral framework.

After months of fighting, the Allies reduced the German defensive lines one by one and Rome fell on June 5, 1944. The Wehrmacht then withdrew farther north. In June, I. and III./JG 53 went to fight in the RVT, abandoning Italy in turn. I. and II./JG 77 as well as I. /JG 4 remained in the northern Italy.

On August 15, the Allies launched Operation *Dragoon*, the landing in Provence, south of France. To reinforce the pitifully weak Luftwaffe in the area (reduced to JG 200, an operational training unit only), II./JG 77 was transferred from northern Italy to southern France. However, the Gruppe could do little and returned some ten days later. As with most rapid re-deployments of this type there was a shortage of transport capacity. The Bf 109s carried additional "passengers"; one or two mechanics crammed into the rear fuselage. After flying a handful of sorties over the "invasion" bridgehead for no tangible result, the Gruppe was ordered back to northern Italy.

Shortly after the return of II. /JG 77, I. /JG 4 left for the Reich, followed a little while later by II. and I./JG 77. Alongside the RSI

Seen on the wing of his Gustav in Italy, Ofw. Hans Kornatz was a rare "first to last" survivor with I./JG 53. He was awarded the German Cross in Gold in March 1944. On April 10, 1945, as Staffelkapitän 1./JG 53, he was shot down over Vienna but managed a successful belly-landing. He returned some 36 victories.

Desertion over Italy, July 25, 1944

At 15:35 eight Bf 109s of 1./JG 4 and eight others from 3./JG 4 (all equipped with supplementary fuel tanks) took off from Maniago under the leadership of Lt. Harry Mayer. The group notably included Uffz. René Darbois. This French native of Metz had decided to desert at the first opportunity. Shortly after takeoff, respecting strict radio silence, Darbois placed himself ahead of his chief and indicated by gestures that he was ill and had to land as quickly as possible. Mayer consulted his maps and told his pilot that he could land at Treviso, which they were overflying at that moment. Darbois detached himself from the formation and took the direction shown. Noticing that his wingman had followed him, he signalled to him that he should rejoin the formation as quickly as possible, which he did. Out of sight of his comrades, the Frenchman made a turn, headed for Venice, disconnected his radio and made several changes of direction and altitude to deceive any radar tracking him. Waggling his wings to signal his intention to land, he landed without incident at Santa Maria, an aerodrome occupied by the USAAF.

Two views of the 1./JG 4 Bf 109 G-6 flown by the deserter Uffz. René Darbois. Although enrolled in the Luftwaffe and by all accounts an excellent Bf 109 pilot, Darbois—born in Metz—considered himself to be French first and foremost. Later in the war he flew P-47 Thunderbolts with the Free French Groupe de Chasse II/18 against the German Atlantic coast "pockets" and post-war was a member of the French aerobatic team, the Patrouille d'Etampes. Training on helicopters in the U.S., he later flew over 500 medevac missions and served at Dien Bien Phu. Profoundly disturbed by his experiences, he committed suicide on his return from Indochina.

Following the Allied landings in Provence, II./JG 77 flew to France. The ground staff completed the transfer in Italian Savoia transports pressed into Luftwaffe service to make up the shortfall in equipment.

fighter units, the Luftwaffe left only a few specialized reconnaissance or ground support units in northern Italy. The Tagjagd had now completely deserted the peninsula.

In the first part of the year, III./JG 27 had stood guard over the Aegean Sea. Gradually, fighter units were recalled in the Reich but, to protect maritime traffic in the Aegean, 7./JG 27 with increased manpower was stationed between Rhodes and Athens. The Staffel evacuated the area in May and was sent to Normandy.

7./JG 27 was the last German fighter unit in Greece. Five of its inexperienced, and boyish, pilots are seated on the front of a Bf 109 G-6 at Maleme, Crete. From left: Uffz. Franz Büsen (killed on June 9, 1944 near Caen), Uffz. Gerhard Siegling (killed on May 14, 1944 in the Aegean, two victories), Uffz. Hans Giese (injured on June 14, 1944 near Caen, one victory), Austrian Uffz. Johann Penz (captured on July 2, 1944 near Bayeux, two victories), and Uffz. Karl Schaffhauser (killed on March 2, 1945 over Germany, two victories).

Fw 190 D-9 (W.Nr. 210194) was belly-landed by Fw. Werner Hohenberg of I./JG 2 during the *Bodenplatte* operation, the Luftwaffe's attack on Allied airfields on New Year's Day 1945. The 95 Fw 190s and Bf 109s of JG 2 encountered a storm of American antiaircraft fire south of Aix-la-Chapelle shortly after getting airborne on the ill-fated mission and 15 aircraft, including at least six Doras, were shot down.

1945

On January 1, 1945 the Luftwaffe launched Operation *Bodenplatte* targeting aerodromes in France, the Netherlands, and Belgium. Constantly postponed due to the weather, *Bodenplatte* took place by chance on New Year's Day when it should have been launched at the beginning of the Ardennes offensive. The Allied air forces, deprived of Ultra information, were caught napping. It was, in absolute terms, a German victory, but a Pyrrhic victory at best since 213 Luftwaffe pilots were lost.

Some of them were certainly *Nachwuchs*; they would undoubtedly have been ineffective in combat and quickly shot down. Flying the *Bodenplatte* operation, they at least had the chance of

Lt. Heinrich Hackler had flown with III./JG 77 since 1941, taking part in all the Gruppe's campaigns. He had 56 victories in total but had only received the Knight's Cross in August 1944. On January 1, 1945, he failed to return from the raid on Antwerp. His body was discovered in the Netherlands in his Bf 109 some 60 years later.

Gefr. Walter Wagner (5./JG 4) was forced to make an emergency landing on January 1 at the controls of his Fw 190 A-8 White 11 at St. Trond in Belgium. His machine was recovered and repainted by the USAAF's 404th FG, and while the machine was taxied, it was not flown.

destroying some enemy aircraft. But among the missing were two Geschwaderkommodoren, six Gruppenkommandeure and ten Staffelkapitäne, including three Knight's Cross bearers. Günther Specht leading JG 11 was shot down by American antiaircraft fire near the airfield at As (Belgian Limburg). He had 34 victories to his credit, including 17 *Viermots*. Few Allied airmen were killed while their machines could soon be replaced. In fact, since Normandy, air warfare had turned into a *Materialschlacht*, the numerical superiority of Allied material simply overwhelming the numerically weaker Wehrmacht.

It seems that at the end of 1944, aware of the Tagjagd's disproportionate but futile efforts, Hitler proposed to dissolve the fighter arm and transfer all its personnel into a reinforced Flak arm, accelerating the production of antiaircraft guns. This idea, which would have saved the lives of hundreds of young pilots, was resoundingly rejected by the Luftwaffe hierarchy. But as defeat approached, dissension appeared and broke out into what has been pretentiously and inaccurately described as the "revolt of the generals." Led by Lützow and most probably by Galland (who fell into disgrace), the aces of the old guard filed a manifesto in January denouncing Göring for the "failure of the Luftwaffe." While the charge was simplistic, it was not without some foundation. On the other hand, no one seems to have asked the fundamental question: how could an air force rapidly built up from almost nothing hold its own throughout five years of a global conflict? In the end the dissidents could not be stopped or executed but most were transferred. Many went with Galland to JV 44 and to a lesser extent JG 7, both units equipped with the Me 262 jet. Victories would continue to be won by these *Experten* but the 262 came too late to influence the conflict.

Another revolutionary fighter was the He 162, the *Volksjäger* (people's fighter). Tested in combat by JG 1, and flown by Lt. Gerd Hanf of 4./JG 1 after 9./JG 77 was renamed, it did not have time to become fully operational.

On February 7, 1945, Kommandeur III./JG 77, Maj. Armin Köhler (right), was awarded the Knight's Cross for 40 victories. His tally included 13 *Viermots.*

Despite the terrible conditions prevailing, the last months of war were still eventful for the Tagjagd. Up to May 10, 1945, 35 Knight's Crosses (including five posthumously), eight Oak Leaves and four Swords were issued, the last honors bestowed by the Luftwaffe on those who fought with determination until the end. In return, 23 Knight's Cross bearers died during these last few months of the war, while several others were seriously wounded. Aces appeared and disappeared anonymously. Despite this gloomy atmosphere of near defeat, morale paradoxically remained quite high within the Luftwaffe. According to one member of III./JG 77: "We had enough food and fuel to keep repelling Soviet aircraft. We were therefore living without worrying too much about tomorrow."

In Hungary JG 52 continued to resist—now flying and fighting against both Americans and Russians—as Heinz "Esau" Ewald of JG 52 recalled in his memoir, *Wo wir sind ist immer oben* (*Wherever we are, we are always on top*):

> Veszprem, Hungary, March 1, 1945—Alarm! scramble!—Eduard "Edi" Pitzl, Gerd Hauter, Anton Kellmeier and myself, Heinz Ewald, get airborne. Over Stulhweissenburg we come under fire from Russian and then German antiaircraft artillery. Something's up!
>
> "*Achtung,*" I call over the radio, "*viele Indianer vor uns! Frage Victor?*"—"lots of bandits up ahead of us, do you copy?" *For heaven's sake Esau,* I think to myself, *there's at least 20 silver birds, dark American stars on the wings and fuselage, right in our path.* "Esau to Edi, take your wingman and climb for altitude and don't attack until you have height advantage—we'll split up now, copied." I get a "Roger" back—*Roger! Esau,* I say to myself, *no doubt some of these boys will try and get in behind us and make mischief.* My wingman Paul Slodczyk was already covering me and we now climbed in a northwesterly direction in order to get into a position to dive down on the Amis. While we were straining for height I called up "Jumbo" our controller and reported contact with a large group of Americans in the hope that he might be able to launch another Schwarm but we were out of luck—it was just the four of us against more than 20 of them ... combat against superior numbers had become our daily bread and so it would be today. The Amis were now over Lake Balaton at around 3,000 meters. They were getting closer to our field. They were visibly not too concerned about us, which I was glad about. I had cut off their escape route and was now about 2,000 meters higher up and almost directly over the top of them. At the same time as I called out "*Pauke,*

> *Pauke!*" ("Tally-ho!"), I threw my kite over onto its wingtip and dove down into the attack! Almost simultaneously Edi Pitzl dove down and opened up on the Mustang flying on the left flank of the formation—a hit; the silver bird spun away out of control streaming smoke and a chute billowed out. I confirmed his victory and congratulated him just as "my" *Sibervogel*, my silver bird, loomed large in my sight! Closing rapidly from astern, I opened up—my first salvo streaked wide as the Mustang pilot threw his stick forward just as I squeezed the firing button! My wingman also overshot. Couldn't be helped! My "Me" was now halfway over on its back pulling hard into a tight curve. This was no firing position but I was managing to stay on my opponent's tail. Suddenly a volley of tracers split the air ahead of us—another mad Ami was letting go with all he had … right into our circle. It turned out that this Texas cowboy—who no doubt practiced his sharpshooting on whiskey glasses in the saloon bar—must have scored some hits as a short while later my engine started to cough and misfire. Meanwhile the Mustang pilot was pulling a tighter and tighter turn, still with two Messerschmitt boys on his tail, juddering on the edge of the stall and streaming contrails from their wingtips. I gave him another salvo and then another and saw a couple of lightning flashes on his machine. Then suddenly he pulled up and in a fraction of a second I pulled back hard on the stick, my Me shuddered, and I got off two more short bursts. The Mustang's controls had been damaged—he went into a gentle turn and now all my rounds were walking into his fuselage and wings. As I broke off—almost ramming my wingman—there was an explosion in the Mustang's engine, pieces of cowling and metal skin whirled off into the slipstream and he streamed a trail of thick dark smoke. "Esau—*Abschuss!*" But now the other Americans were circling at a watchful distance—like laughing hyenas. Up to now—apart from the Texas shooter—they had, thank God, not got involved in the fight.

Three P-51s chased Ewald's G-10/U4 (W.Nr. 610964) as far as Veszprem. At the controls of his lame and smoking "Me," Ewald's thoughts turned to comrade and 136-victory Knight's Cross bearer, Lt. Fönnekold, who had been finished off by P-51s as he had tried to carry out an emergency landing in Hungary. He let down to low altitude hoping that the P-51s would be scared off by the flak—his maneuver resulted in his Messerschmitt coming under fire from the airfield defenses. With his aircraft taking hits and suddenly feeling nose-heavy, Ewald had just enough altitude to bail out over the side of the cockpit, immediately tugging on the ripcord. Even in his 'chute he came under fire—German troops disembarking from a train in the vicinity of the airfield opening up on what they thought was a Russian pilot swinging in his harness as he was later told by eyewitnesses. He came down some four kilometers from the airfield with a hard landing. Even spreadeagled on the ground, Ewald's ordeal was not over—he was approached by Hungarian workers shouting, "*Ruski kaputt!*"

Lt. Heinz "Esau" Ewald at the controls of his Bf 109 G-10 (W.Nr. 61048) White 3 of II./JG 52, Veszprem, February 4, 1945.

In wintry conditions, Kommandeur I./JG 53 Erich Hartmann climbs down from his Bf 109 G-6 Black Double Chevron at Veszprem, Hungary, following a combat sortie on February 20, 1945.

Man, Esau—*die wollen dich umbringen!* They're all trying to kill you! I drew my service revolver and started firing wildly over their heads. As my comrade Sachsenberg put it: "You poor little sod, Esau—first shot down by your own flak, then shot at by German troops, even our Hungarian allies were looking to knock your block off with their pickaxes!

During this fight Uffz. Paul Slodzyk's Bf 109 G-14/U4 (W.Nr. 512613) was shot down in flames southwest of Veszprem, while Uffz. Helmut Rudzinski managed to force-land his G-6 (W.Nr. 442047) at Plattensee. Fw Eduard Pitzl successfully bailed out of his G-10 (W.Nr. 610955) over Lovas.

On January 14, 1945, 911 USAF B-17s and B-24s escorted by 860 fighters bombed oil facilities scattered across central Germany. Clear blue skies offered unlimited visibility, denying the Germans the opportunity of a surprise attack. The result was another bloodbath, one that cost the Luftwaffe 139 pilots. Of the Geschwader which took part in the attack, JG 300 suffered most heavily—with 39 pilots missing or killed in action. III. Gruppe lost Ofhr. Klaus Grothues who plunged into the ground in his G-14/AS Yellow 2—with 17 victories he was the last ace of III./JG 300. Only ten Flying Fortresses were claimed but German losses amounted to almost half the force committed.

For many German fighter pilots, the war was virtually over. There was little or no future or hope. Many had lost their loved ones in the systematic bombings of German cities; others could not return to their home towns, deep behind Soviet lines in eastern Germany. It was among these ranks that volunteers for the *letzter Aufgebot*, the supreme sacrifice, could be found. Some trained for ramming attacks against Allied bombers, others would participate in suicide missions against enemy ground columns, while others would dive their aircraft loaded with explosives into the Elbe and the Oder bridges.

Another view of Hartmann's I./JG 53 Gustav seen here on February 4, 1945, with the so-called "tulip-petal" decoration around the nose and red heart under the cockpit. He had just returned his 337th victory as witnessed by his wingman Lt. Erich Sommavilla.

1./JG 54 pilot Fw Karl-Heinz "Heino" Cordes survived the war, flying his last sorties over Courland in 1945 where he was awarded the *Ehrenpokal*—honor globlet—for outstanding performance in combat. With some 62 victories, he was one of the highest-scoring pilots never to receive the Knight's Cross. Here he is seated on the spinner of his Fw 190 White 1 of 1./JG 54 at Rijelbitzi, May 1943.

The Russians had reached the Oder just 60 miles from Berlin by late January 1945. The *Jagdflieger* suddenly had more pressing concerns than shooting down enemy bombers. Many fighter Gruppen, including all four Gruppen of JG 300, were deployed to the Oder Front in short order and flew sortie after sortie from airfields such as Liegnitz, Schönfeld-Seifersdorf, and Lüben—hazardous low-level strafing and bombing attacks—against Soviet columns for which the pilots had received little or no training. Facilities were rudimentary and runways and airfields were pitted, rutted and laced with large puddles. The weather was mostly bad: snow showers, mist, and fog. When there was visibility, the pilots could see Soviet columns that stretched away to the horizon, their progress marked by columns of smoke.

Some authors have maintained that the Luftwaffe actually gained a measure of air superiority over the Eastern Front during the spring of 1945. However, operating for the most part from makeshift airfields, the German fighters lacked practically everything: fuel, ammunition, spares, fuel bowsers and at times even ground crews. Some were already too close to the front and only just managed to evade the fast-advancing Red Army. The situation was beyond retrieval—with no communication or early warning systems, most fighter missions were freelance sweeps in the vicinity of their own bases. Early morning recce sweeps were usually mounted to ascertain the exact location of the fluid frontlines. In such primitive conditions offensive operations were out of the question.

While the Fw 190s' ventral racks now toted 250-kg bombs and their 2-cm and 3-cm cannon could inflict

Oblt. Otto Kittel, Staka 2./JG 54, was airborne on February 14 to intercept a formation of Sturmoviks. Near Tukum his Fw 190 A-8 (W.Nr. 690282) Black 1 was hit by a gunner's return fire and plunged from low altitude into the ground, leaving him no chance. He was credited with 267 kills, which made him the fourth-highest Luftwaffe ace and the highest-scoring Luftwaffe ace to be killed in action.

heavy losses on soft-skinned vehicles, horse-drawn columns and even tanks, it was often difficult to pick out valid targets on roads clogged with refugees fleeing west ahead of the Soviet advance. Red Army columns also quickly adopted the practice of using streams of refugees as human shields.

On Wednesday, January 31, JG 4 flew only 22 sorties, mostly over Küstrin. The Fw 190 of Fw. Alfred Jacobs (8.(Sturm)/JG 4) took hits from Soviet light flak which damaged the rudder. Jacobs takes up the story:

> Neuhausen near Cottbus was to be the end of the line for me. The weather had closed in—snow, sleet, and heavy low-hanging clouds kept those pilots that had not been trained on instruments on the ground. I was fortunate in that I usually flew my recce and strafing sorties on my own. There was no front line as such—the only indication that I was over enemy-held territory were the streams of light flak that rose to meet me. Panje-mounted [Panje is a type of Polish horse] columns were rolling westward across a landscape blanketed by a shroud of snow. In the woods wisps of smoke betrayed the presence of numerous campfires. There was no way of stopping this tidal wave with our onboard weapons—our task was hopeless. I nonetheless flew a firing pass along one column and destroyed supply carts and wagons but took a direct hit from ground fire in the tailplane. The rudder was jammed in such a fashion that I only got back to the airfield by flying wide circles. I made a successful belly-landing. Later that day I went to collect a new Fw 190 from Cottbus—selecting an unarmored machine from the many standing forlornly in the woods around the plant.

Karl-Heinz Kabus of 3./JG11 based at Strausberg to the east of Berlin reported:

> February 8 was the first time that I flew a sortie with a 250-kg bomb slung under the belly of my 190. We flew many similar sorties over the following weeks against ground troops in the vicinity of Zellin, Mohrin, Pyritz (east of the Oder), and during early March against the Soviet pontoon bridge at Göritz south of Küstrin. From now on we fighter pilots were employed almost exclusively as *Jagdbombenflieger*—fighter-bombers. The bridge at Göritz gave us a lot of trouble. We were told it was especially important since it was the only one capable of taking the weight of the heavy Josef Stalin tanks and we were tasked with destroying it ... without much success. We had been trained as fighter pilots after all. We hit everything round about except for the bridge itself. Otherwise I recall the enormous streams of refugees, even to the east of the Oder.

Karl-Heinz Kabus of 3./JG11.

Along the Baltic, German defensive efforts in the face of the Russian onslaught were largely focused around a series of pockets and *Festungen* or "fortresses." In March 1945, Lt. Eberhard Burath was appointed Staffelkapitän of 9./JG 51. He recorded his seventh, and last, victory on March 22, when he shot down a Pe-2, a feat for which Kommandeur Brendel awarded him the Iron Cross 1st Class. Burath recalled:

> on March 29, III. Gruppe moved to Littausdorf on Samland [Sambia or Kaliningrad Peninsula]. The airfield came under constant attack from Soviet bombers. The western half of the peninsula was still in German hands while the Russians were still besieging the city of Königsberg which finally fell on April 9, 1945. There was little fuel for flying—*der Sprit wird knapp*—only 1,000 liters of fuel per day and per machine—given the Bf 109's fuel tank capacity of 400 liters, that was just enough for two sorties.

On the Western Front the Eighth Air Force launched a full-strength raid against synthetic fuel plants on March 2, 1945. JGs 300 and 301 both managed to commit all four Gruppen for what would prove to be the last time for a total of nearly 200 machines airborne. The II./JG 301 Doras suffered devastating losses running into P-51s north of Magdeburg and for just one B-17 claim no fewer than eight II. Gruppe pilots were killed including Lt. Walter Kropp of 8. Staffel at the controls of Red 1.

Elsewhere the Allies mounted the impressive *Varsity* operation to cross the Rhine on March 24, 1945. The catastrophic air battles that took place that day saw I./JG 300 set upon by 353rd FG P-51s near Göttingen. Seventeen-victory ace Fw Alfred Büthe of 3. Staffel was shot down but managed to bail out—in agony, his legs riddled with rounds fired by pursuing Mustangs. He died of his injuries later that day in hospital. March 24 was one of the last days of combat for JG 300 against USAAF fighters. The pilots of JG 300, JG 2 and JG 26 would clash with increasing frequency with the tactical air forces—Ninth Air Force, First Tactical Air Force (P) and Second Tactical Air Force—supporting the advancing Allied armies.

Oblt. Helmut Rüffler led 9./JG 51 after Burath returned to the Stab JG 51. He was awarded the Knight's Cross on December 23, 1944 for 63 victories. He had previously flown in JG 3 and during February 1945 trained on the Me 262 before spending the last two months of the war with JG 51. He survived with some 88 victories.

Kommandeur I./JG 51 Hptm. Günther Schack pictured on April 12, 1945, his face swathed in bandages after being badly burned. He had continued to fly combat sorties. To the right of him is Oblt. Günther Josten (178 victories) and to the left, Oblt. Anton Lindner (73 victories).

On March 26 Oblt. Karl-Wilhelm Hofmann was killed in action having just downed his 44th victim. Despite the terrible attrition, the fighter aces—especially those at the controls of the Fw 190 D-9—could still inflict losses. On March 28, Staffelkapitän 14./JG 26, Oblt. Hans Dortenmann, and his Staffel bounced RAF Tempests in the vicinity of Münster, Dortenmann claiming his 31st kill. He achieved some 18 victories on the type and was one of the leading aces on the Fw 190 D-9. He was awarded the Knight's Cross in late April 1945, credited with around 38 victories.

Having been shot down and wounded on December 24, 1944, Hubert Engst of 6./JG 300 rejoined his Staffel during 1945 and flew sorties to the end of the war. During March and April 1945 he described in his diary the rearguard retreat of II./JG 300 through southern Germany—ceaseless *Tiefangriffe* strafing sorties against American tank colums. He had harsh words for his superiors including his Kommandeur who rarely flew during this period due to "sickness." On April 9, 1945, Engst was set upon by several P-51 D Mustangs in the vicinity of Bayreuth. He took to his parachute, unharmed. In the first week of May 1945 what was left of JG 300 was ordered to fall back on Prague—Engst personally witnessed the unit's Fw 190 Doras get airborne for the last airfield transfer of the war.

Oblt. Hans Dortenmann in the cockpit of Black 1 (W.Nr. 210003), an early-production Dora-9. He flew this aircraft –despite it being plagued with engine problems—through to May 5, 1945 before blowing it up to prevent it falling into British hands. Although the Staffel number was "1," its color changed through red, black, and yellow as III./JG 54 was redesignated IV./JG 26.

Fw 190 A-8 Yellow 9 flown by Fw. Hannes Theis of 6./JG 300. Theis flew his first *Jabo* mission in the Gotha–Eisenach–Kassel sector on April 3, 1945. The inscription "Roter Hahn" ("Red Rooster") is just visible under the cockpit. Theis was credited with around ten kills.

Hubert Engst of 6./JG 300 preparing for a spell of cockpit readiness in FW 190 A-8 *Sturmbock* Yellow 2 (W.Nr 682181). Note the EZ 42 gyroscopic sight above the instrument panel. He was credited with around seven kills and survived the war.

Afterword

The hopelessness and despair of last months of the war did not spare the aces. Günther Lützow disappeared on April 24 near Donauwörth. He had been credited with two new *Luftsiege* at the controls of the Me 262. If details about Lützow's last moments are sketchy there are few doubts about the circumstances of the death of Maj. Heinrich Ehrler—he had announced his imminent suicide over the radio. On April 4, as a member of JG 7 and having achieved eight jet victories, he voluntarily rammed a B-17 near Stendal. As Kommodore JG 5, Maj. Ehrler had recently been convicted by a court martial for his "part" in the fiasco that had resulted in the destruction of the *Tirpitz* in a Norwegian fjord, a decision that certainly weighed heavily on him.

On Saturday April 7, 1945 the Luftwaffe launched Operation *Elbe,* a mass "suicide" sortie flown by more than 150 young pilots for what was planned as a one-way ramming mission against an American bomber formation in the region of Lake Steinhuder. Although the pilots were to attempt to bail out after directing their lightly armed 109s into a bomber, the chances of successfully achieving this must have been slim. On the American side this encounter with a large and potentially determined force of German fighters was to come as an unpleasant surprise. Ultimately, neither the numbers committed nor the courage of this group of fanatical or desperate young pilots could inflict the levels of hoped-for losses. The bomber escort and the bombers' defensive firepower accounted for large numbers of the "rammers" before they were able to fly their fighters into their targets. After an air battle that lasted some 45 minutes, 15 German fighters returned to their airfields. In total the

Uffz. Josef Stenner of 14./JG 300—on his Bf 109 G-10—survived the war despite volunteering for the "Sonderkommando" *Elbe* ramming mission of March 1945.

"Sonderkommando" claimed around 20 bombers at the most. Despite this setback, the idea of deploying suicide pilots—German kamikazes—had taken hold in the upper echelons of the Luftwaffe. JG 4—or what was left of the Geschwader—would be closely associated with the follow-up to the *Elbe* mission: Operation *Samurai*.

On April 17, 1945, just a matter of a fortnight before the end of the war, Hptm. Johannes Kaufmann, Staffelkapitän 9./JG 4, flew an escort sortie for so-called German kamikaze *Flieger*:

> Kamikaze *Flieger* were suicide pilots dispatched on sorties from which there would be with no return, their 109s crammed with explosives. Airborne from Mark Zwuschen, we orbited over Jüterbog where our charges were taxiing out. At the controls of their heavily loaded machines, these pilots didn't even wear parachutes—they had nothing they could fall back on. Their takeoff runs were laborious and long and the laden machines strained for altitude. I recall that one of my charges appeared reluctant to go through with his mission. He closed on me several times at altitude before finally apparently resolving to throw his aircraft at the target—I watched as he fell away in a steep dive and impacted in a huge ball of flame. On our return it was as much as we could do to report, "Targets hit!"

JG 4 flew some of its last ground-attack missions of the war around the capital and the area of Neustrelitz on April 29. Uffz. Manfred Kudell of 8.(Sturm)/JG 4 was one pilot who paid the price, airborne over Berlin at 08:45 that morning:

> Between April 14 and 29, I flew 29 combat sorties over Berlin and its suburbs. These were mostly *Jabo* ground-attack flights but we also flew plenty of *Schlachtflieger* ground-attack escort missions over the Kremmen–Nauen sector in an attempt to slow the encirclement of the capital. Over Berlin itself we generally ran into Yak fighters. During the last days we flew such a high rate of sorties that there was little

A magnificent shot of Dora-13 Yellow 10 (W.Nr 836017) assigned to the last Kommodore of JG 26, 63-victory ace Maj. Franz Götz. This was one of only two D-13s confirmed built and in service by April 7, 1945 in this W.Nr. block.

Lt. Kurt Tanzer was appointed Staffelkapitän of 13./JG 51 on April 12, 1945 and led the unit's Doras on a Mistel escort sortie flown against the Oder bridges that same day. Here he is seen deep in thought on the field at Parchim prior to making his final flight in an Fw 190 Dora. The unit's handful of Doras flew into Flensburg on May 8, 1945 to surrender. Comparatively little is known about Kurt Tanzer's fighter pilot career, while his victory total is unlikely to have been as high as 143, the figure usually quoted.

time to properly plan them, which meant that they were mostly ineffectual. I was airborne—with my Schwarm—on April 29. My Fw 190 carried a 250-kg bomb and I had orders to target Soviet tanks heading for the Chancellery. There was little hope of us successfully carrying out this mission given the huge pall of smoke that shrouded the city—it was impossible to make out anything on the ground clearly. In fact, only those pilots—such as myself—who knew the city and could pick out landmarks to navigate by were dispatched. Each pilot was assigned to attack a street in the vicinity of the Reichskanzlei [Reich Chancellery]. My objective was Stresemannstrasse. Airborne from Rechlin, we swept in over the Reichskanzlei at rooftop height. We had no radio or visual contact with each other and Berlin was one huge cloud of smoke. We had no idea where our own troops were. We dropped our ordnance and turned onto a northerly heading in an attempt to reach Rechlin. As I came out through the clouds of smoke, I was immediately set upon by Soviet fighters and despite my desperate maneuvers, had to bail out at 3,000 meters. I landed—badly burned—in the midst of street fighting. I was captured by Russian soldiers.

Line-up of Fw 190 A-8 and Dora 9s of IV./JG 51 at Flensburg after surrendering in early May 1945.

Sachsenberg Schwarm aces—the so-called "Papagei-Staffel"—tasked with covering takeoffs and landings of the Me 262-equipped elite Jagdverband 44 commanded by Adolf Galland. Led by Lt. Heinz Sachsenberg (second from right, wearing his Knight's Cross), a JG 52 veteran with 104 victories, the colorful Dora-9s of this ad-hoc unit were flown by Hptm. Waldemar Wübke, a Battle of Britain veteran with JG 54 (to Sachsenberg's left), and Oblt. Klaus Faber (to Sachsenberg's right), a former JG 27 Bf 109 pilot in Africa. Faber had been captured by the British but subsequently escaped. He reportedly achieved the JV 44 Doras' only victory in combat, shooting down a P-47 during a courier flight on May 3, 1945. The pilots are pictured in front of Red 3 of JV 44 in April 1945.

Gruppenkommandeur II./SG 2 Karl Kennel was one of a number of Schlachtgeschwader ground-attack pilots who claimed large numbers of Soviet aircraft shot down. This is his Fw 190 A-8 after he deliberately crash-landed the machine on the American-held airfield at Kitzingen on May 8, 1945. Over the course of nearly 1,000 operational flights, Kennel claimed 34 victories.

Hartmann seen on his return to Germany after ten years of Soviet captivity.

The Surrender of JG 52, May 1945

During the spring of 1945, elements of I. and III./ JG 52 operated from Deutsch (Nemecky) Brod in Czech territory. While the personnel of both Gruppen subsequently surrendered to the Americans, they were handed over to the Russians and endured long years of captivity post-war. Elsewhere the personnel of II./JG 52 had flown to southern Germany to surrender to American forces and were thus the only members of this Geschwader to escape the Soviet camps. It was from Deutsch Brod that Erich Hartmann returned the last of his victories, probably at the controls of his Erla-built Bf 109 G-10 seen on the occasion of his 350th kill. However, the Bf 109 G-10 was not the last variant of the Bf 109 to see combat. Photographic evidence from JG 52's surrender at Deutsch Brod indicates that the Stab JG 52 had received a number of Bf 109 K-4s.

While high-ranking and highly decorated pilots invariably received the latest equipment in an effort to maintain an advantage over their adversaries, conditions in German manufacturing in early 1945 were chaotic with slave labor and large numbers of concentration camp inmates forced into production duties. Inevitably machines were leaving factories—including *Waldwerke* (forest factories)—with little or no quality control. A Bf 109 pilot ferrying K-4s recorded that his aircraft were minus instruments, even oxygen. So it is unlikely that Hartmann ever flew the variant.

Surrendered Bf 109 G-10s of II./JG 52, May 1945.

Glossary

Abschuss	a kill, a downing (pl. *Abschüsse*)
Bereitschaft	readiness
BG/BW	Bombardment Group/Bombardment Wing (USAAF)
Einsatz	operational mission (pl. *Einsätze*)
Experte	ace (pl. *Experten*)
Feindberührung	contact with the enemy
Feindflug	a flight over enemy territory (pl. *Feindflüge*)
FG	Fighter Group (USAAF)
Fhr.	Fähnrich (Fahnenjunker)/Flight Officer
Flugplatz	airfield (pl. *Flugplätze*)
Frontflug	a sortie, combat sortie
Frontflugspange	operational missions clasp for a specified number of sorties
Führeranlass	special decree
Fw.	Feldwebel/Technical Sergeant
Gefr.	Gefreiter/Aircraftman/Airman
Geschwader	a wing/group, comprising 90–120 aircraft (pl. Geschwader)
Gruppe	autonomous Luftwaffe group, smaller than a USAAF group/RAF wing but larger than a squadron (pl. Gruppen)
Hptm.	Hauptmann/Captain/ Flight Lieutenant
HSS	*Herausschuss*, lit. "shoot-out"—the separation of a bomber from its formation
IAD/IAP	Fighter Aviation Division/Regiment (Soviet)
Jabo	dive-bomber, or fighter-bomber
JaFü	Jagdfliegerführer, commander Fighter forces
Jagdflieger	fighter pilot
Jagdgeschwader	a fighter wing/group, comprising 90–120 aircraft (abbr. JG)
Jagdegruppe	a fighter group (abbr. JGr.)
Kette	a flight of three aircraft
Lt.	Leutnant/Second Lieutenant/Pilot Officer
Luftsieg	air victory (pl. *Luftsiege*)
Maj.	Major/Squadron Leader
Obfw.	Oberfeldwebel/Flight Sergeant/Master Sergeant
Oblt.	Oberleutenant/First Lieutenant/Flying Officer
Obstlt.	Oberstleutenant
Ofhr.	Oberfahnrich/ Flight Sergeant
Rotte	a pair of aircraft, lit. pack (pl. Rotten)
RVT	Reichsverteidigung, air defense of the Reich
Schlageter	JG 26, named after Albert Leo Schlageter
Schwarm	a flight, lit. a swarm, comprising 4–6 aircraft (pl. Schwärme)
Sitzbereitschaft	cockpit readiness
Sqn	Squadron
Stab	Staff Flight
Staffel	a flight squadron/echelon comprising 9–12 aircraft (pl. Staffeln)
Staka	abbr. of Staffelkapitän
Tagjagd	day fighter arm of the WWII Luftwaffe
Tagjäger	day fighter/s
Uffz.	Unteroffizier/Corporal (RAF)/Sergeant (USAAF)
Ufw.	Unterfeldwebel/Sergeant
Viermot	four-engined bomber, lit. four engines
W.Nr.	*Werk Nummer,* factory number (of an aircraft)
Zerstörer	heavy fighter, fighter-bomber
ZG	Zerstörergeschwader, heavy/destroyer squadron

Bibliography

Aders, G., *Jagdgeschwader 51 Mölders* (Motorbuch, 1999)

Bergström, C., *Black Cross–Red Star, Stalingrad to Kuban*, Vol. 4 (Vaktel books, 2019)

Eriksson, P., *Alarmstart East* (Amberley, 2017)

Lorant, J-Y., *Jagdgeschwader 300: A Chronicle of a Fighter Geschwader in the Defence of the Reich* (2 vols trans. Neil Page, Eagle Editions, 2005)

__________, *Le Focke Wulf 190* (Editions Larivière, 1983: French text)

Mombeeck, Eric, *Jagdgeschwader 2: In the Skies of France* (Vol. I: Porte d'Hoves, self-published, trans. Neil Page)

__________, *Jagdgeschwader 26: The Abbeville Boys* (Luftwaffe Gallery unit Special: Porte d'Hoves, self-published, trans. Neil Page)

__________, *Jagdgeschwader 5: Fighters of the Midnight Sun* (Luftwaffe Gallery unit Special: Porte d'Hoves, self-published, trans. Neil Page)

__________, *Jagdgeschwader 54: The Green Hearts* (Luftwaffe Gallery Unit Special: Porte d'Hoves, self-published, trans. Neil Page)

__________, *Jagdgeschwader 77: Fighting on All Fronts* (Luftwaffe Gallery Unit Special: Porte d'Hoves, self-published, trans. Neil Page)

__________, *Storming the Bombers: A Chronicle of JG 4* (self-published, 2 vols, trans. Neil Page)

Obermaier, E., *Die Ritterkreuzträger der Luftwaffe* (Verlag Dieter Hoffmann)

Page, Neil, *Aircraft in Profile: Focke Wulf 190 A* (Scale Aircraft Modelling, November 2002)

__________, *Sturmgruppen 1944: Focke Wulf 190 Bomber Destroyers* (Scale Aircraft Modelling, March 2001)

Prien, J., *Die Jagdfliegerverbände der Deutschen Luftwaffe* (purple series) (Struve Druck/Rogge, multiple volumes)

__________, *Geschichte des Jagdgeschwader 77* (Struve Druck, 4 vols)

Roba, Jean-Louis, *La chasse de Jour allemande en Roumanie* (Bucharest, 1994)

__________, *Les As de la chasse de Jour allemande, 1939–1945* (ETAI, 2012)

Rodeike, P., *Focke Wulf Jagdflugzeug 190* (Struve Druck, Eutin 1998. ISBN 3-923 457-44-8: German text)

Schmoll, P., *Me 109: Produktion und Einsatz* (MZ Verlag, 2017 ISBN: 9783866463561)

Schmidt, Erik, *Black Tulip* (Casemate, 2020)

Stipdonk, P., *Das Jagdgeschwader 51 Mölders* (VDM, 1996)

Index